6. Enter your class ID code to join a class.

### IF YOU HAVE A CLASS CODE FROM YOUR TEACHER

a. Enter your class code and click **Next**

b. Once you have joined a class, you will be able to use the Discussion Board and Email tools.

c. To enter this code later, choose **Join a Class**.

### IF YOU DO NOT HAVE A CLASS CODE

a. If you do not have a class ID code, click **Skip**

b. You do not need a class ID code to use *iQ Online*.

c. To enter this code later, choose **Join a Class**.

7. Review registration information and click Log In. Then choose your book. Click **Activities** to begin using *iQ Online*.

### IMPORTANT

- After you register, the next time you want to use *iQ Online*, go to www.iQOnlinePractice.com and log in with your email address and password.
- The online content can be used for 12 months from the date you register.
- For help, please contact customer service: eltsupport@oup.com.

## WHAT IS iQ ONLINE?

All new activities provide essential skills **practice** and support.

Vocabulary and Grammar **games** immerse you in the language and provide even more practice.

Authentic, engaging **videos** generate new ideas and opinions on the Unit Question.

Go to the Media Center to download or stream all **student book audio**.

Use the **Discussion Board** to discuss the Unit Question and more.

**Email** encourages communication with your teacher and classmates.

**Automatic grading** gives immediate feedback and tracks progress.

**Progress Reports** show what you have mastered and where you still need more practice.

# SHAPING learning TOGETHER

We would like to acknowledge the teachers from all over the world who participated in the development process and review of the Q series.

**Special thanks to our *Q: Skills for Success* Second Edition Topic Advisory Board**

**Shaker Ali Al-Mohammad**, Buraimi University College, Oman; **Dr. Asmaa A. Ebrahim**, University of Sharjah, U.A.E.; **Rachel Batchilder**, College of the North Atlantic, Qatar; **Anil Bayir**, Izmir University, Turkey; **Flora Mcvay Bozkurt**, Maltepe University, Turkey; **Paul Bradley**, University of the Thai Chamber of Commerce Bangkok, Thailand; **Joan Birrell-Bertrand**, University of Manitoba, MB, Canada; **Karen E. Caldwell**, Zayed University, U.A.E.; **Nicole Hammond Carrasquel**, University of Central Florida, FL, U.S.; **Kevin Countryman**, Seneca College of Applied Arts & Technology, ON, Canada; **Julie Crocker**, Arcadia University, NS, Canada; **Marc L. Cummings**, Jefferson Community and Technical College, KY, U.S.; **Rachel DeSanto**, Hillsborough Community College Dale Mabry Campus, FL, U.S.; **Nilüfer Ertürkmen**, Ege University, Turkey; **Sue Fine**, Ras Al Khaimah Women's College (HCT), U.A.E.; **Amina Al Hashami**, Nizwa College of Applied Sciences, Oman; **Stephan Johnson**, Nagoya Shoka Daigaku, Japan; **Sean Kim**, Avalon, South Korea; **Gregory King**, Chubu Daigaku, Japan; **Seran Küçük**, Maltepe University, Turkey; **Jonee De Leon**, VUS, Vietnam; **Carol Lowther**, Palomar College, CA, U.S.; **Erin Harris-MacLead**, St. Mary's University, NS, Canada; **Angela Nagy**, Maltepe University, Turkey; **Huynh Thi Ai Nguyen**, Vietnam; **Daniel L. Paller**, Kinjo Gakuin University, Japan; **Jangyo Parsons**, Kookmin University, South Korea; **Laila Al Qadhi**, Kuwait University, Kuwait; **Josh Rosenberger**, English Language Institute University of Montana, MT, U.S.; **Nancy Schoenfeld**, Kuwait University, Kuwait; **Jenay Seymour**, Hongik University, South Korea; **Moon-young Son**, South Korea; **Matthew Taylor**, Kinjo Gakuin Daigaku, Japan; **Burcu Tezcan-Unal**, Zayed University, U.A.E.; **Troy Tucker**, Edison State College-Lee Campus, FL, U.S.; **Kris Vicca**, Feng Chia University, Taichung; **Jisook Woo**, Incheon University, South Korea; **Dunya Yenidunya**, Ege University, Turkey

**UNITED STATES** **Marcarena Aguilar**, North Harris College, TX; **Rebecca Andrade**, California State University North Ridge, CA; **Lesley Andrews**, Boston University, MA; **Deborah Anholt**, Lewis and Clark College, OR; **Robert Anzelde**, Oakton Community College, IL; **Arlys Arnold**, University of Minnesota, MN; **Marcia Arthur**, Renton Technical College, WA; **Renee Ashmeade**, Passaic County Community College, NJ; **Anne Bachmann**, Clackamas Community College, OR; **Lida Baker**, UCLA, CA; **Ron Balsamo**, Santa Rosa Junior College, CA; **Lori Barkley**, Portland State University, OR; **Eileen Barlow**, SUNY Albany, NY; **Sue Bartch**, Cuyahoga Community College, OH; **Lora Bates**, Oakton High School, VA; **Barbara Batra**, Nassau County Community College, NY; **Nancy Baum**, University of Texas at Arlington, TX; **Rebecca Beck**, Irvine Valley College, CA; **Linda Berendsen**, Oakton Community College, IL; **Jennifer Binckes Lee**, Howard Community College, MD; **Grace Bishop**, Houston Community College, TX; **Jean W. Bodman**, Union County College, NJ; **Virginia Bouchard**, George Mason University, VA; **Kimberley Briesch Sumner**, University of Southern California, CA; **Kevin Brown**, University of California, Irvine, CA; **Laura Brown**, Glendale Community College, CA; **Britta Burton**, Mission College, CA; **Allison L. Callahan**, Harold Washington College, IL; **Gabriela Cambiasso**, Harold Washington College, IL; **Jackie Campbell**, Capistrano Unified School District, CA; **Adele C. Camus**, George Mason University, VA; **Laura Chason**, Savannah College, GA; **Kerry Linder Catana**, Language Studies International, NY; **An Cheng**, Oklahoma State University, OK; **Carole Collins**, North Hampton Community College, PA; **Betty R. Compton**, Intercultural Communications College, HI; **Pamela Couch**, Boston University, MA; **Fernanda Crowe**, Intrax International Institute, CA; **Vicki Curtis**, Santa Cruz, CA; **Margo Czinski**, Washtenaw Community College, MI; **David Dahnke**, Lone Star College, TX; **Gillian M. Dale**, CA; **L. Dalgish**, Concordia College, MN; **Christopher Davis**, John Jay College, NY; **Sherry Davis**, Irvine University, CA; **Natalia de Cuba**, Nassau County Community College, NY; **Sonia Delgadillo**, Sierra College, CA; **Esmeralda Diriye**, Cypress College & Cal Poly, CA; **Marta O. Dmytrenko-Ahrabian**, Wayne State University, MI; **Javier Dominguez**, Central High School, SC; **Jo Ellen Downey-Greer**, Lansing Community College, MI; **Jennifer Duclos**, Boston University, MA; **Yvonne Duncan**, City College of San Francisco, CA; **Paul Dydman**, USC Language Academy, CA; **Anna Eddy**, University of Michigan-Flint, MI; **Zohan El-Gamal**, Glendale Community College, CA; **Jennie Farnell**, University of Connecticut, CT; **Susan Fedors**, Howard Community College, MD; **Valerie Fiechter**, Mission College, CA; **Ashley Fifer**, Nassau County Community College, NY; **Matthew Florence**, Intrax International Institute, CA; **Kathleen Flynn**, Glendale College, CA; **Elizabeth Fonsea**, Nassau County Community College, NY; **Eve Fonseca**, St. Louis Community College, MO; **Elizabeth Foss**, Washtenaw Community College, MI; **Duff C. Galda**, Pima Community College, AZ; **Christiane Galvani**, Houston Community College, TX; **Gretchen Gerber**, Howard Community College, MD; **Ray Gonzalez**, Montgomery College, MD; **Janet Goodwin**, University of California, Los Angeles, CA; **Alyona Gorokhova**, Grossmont College, CA; **John Graney**, Santa Fe College, FL; **Kathleen Green**, Central High School, AZ; **Nancy Hamadou**, Pima Community College-West Campus, AZ; **Webb Hamilton**, De Anza College, San Jose City College, CA; **Janet Harclerode**, Santa Monica Community College, CA; **Sandra Hartmann**, Language and Culture Center, TX; **Kathy Haven**, Mission College, CA; **Roberta Hendrick**, Cuyahoga Community College, OH; **Ginny Heringer**, Pasadena City College, CA; **Adam Henricksen**, University of Maryland, MD; **Carolyn Ho**, Lone Star College-CyFair, TX; **Peter Hoffman**, LaGuardia Community College, NY; **Linda Holden**, College of Lake County, IL; **Jana Holt**, Lake Washington Technical College, WA; **Antonio Iccarino**, Boston University, MA; **Gail Ibele**, University of Wisconsin, WI; **Nina Ito**, American Language Institute, CSU Long Beach, CA; **Linda Jensen**, UCLA, CA; **Lisa Jurkowitz**, Pima Community College, CA; **Mandy Kama**, Georgetown University, Washington, DC; **Stephanie Kasuboski**, Cuyahoga Community College, OH; **Chigusa Katoku**, Mission College, CA; **Sandra Kawamura**, Sacramento City College, CA; **Gail Kellersberger**, University of Houston-Downtown, TX; **Jane Kelly**, Durham Technical Community College, NC; **Maryanne Kildare**, Nassau County Community College, NY; **Julie Park Kim**, George Mason University, VA; **Kindra Kinyon**, Los Angeles Trade-Technical College, CA; **Matt Kline**, El Camino College, CA; **Lisa Kovacs-Morgan**, University of California, San Diego, CA; **Claudia Kupiec**, DePaul University, IL; **Renee La Rue**, Lone Star College-Montgomery, TX; **Janet Langon**, Glendale College, CA; **Lawrence Lawson**, Palomar College, CA; **Rachele Lawton**, The Community College of Baltimore County, MD; **Alice Lee**, Richland College, TX; **Esther S. Lee**, CSUF & Mt. SAC, CA; **Cherie Lenz-Hackett**, University of Washington, WA; **Joy Leventhal**, Cuyahoga Community College, OH; **Alice Lin**, UCI Extension, CA; **Monica Lopez**, Cerritos College, CA; **Dustin Lovell**, FLS International Marymount College, CA; **Carol Lowther**, Palomar College, CA; **Candace Lynch-Thompson**, North Orange County Community College District, CA; **Thi Thi Ma**, City College of San Francisco, CA; **Steve Mac Isaac**, USC Long Academy, CA; **Denise Maduli-Williams**, City College of San Francisco, CA; **Eileen Mahoney**, Camelback High School, AZ; **Naomi Mardock**, MCC-Omaha, NE; **Brigitte Maronde**, Harold Washington College, IL; **Marilyn Marquis**, Laposita College CA; **Doris Martin**, Glendale Community College; Pasadena City College, CA; **Keith Maurice**, University of Texas at Arlington, TX; **Nancy Mayer**, University of Missouri-St. Louis, MO; **Aziah McNamara**, Kansas State University, KS; **Billie McQuillan**, Education Heights, MN; **Karen Merritt**, Glendale Union High School District, AZ; **Holly Milkowart**, Johnson County Community College, KS; **Eric Moyer**, Intrax International Institute, CA; **Gino Muzzatti**, Santa Rosa Junior College, CA; **Sandra Navarro**, Glendale Community College, CA; **Than Nyeinkhin**, ELAC, PCC, CA; **William Nedrow**, Triton College, IL; **Eric Nelson**, University of Minnesota, MN; **Than Nyeinkhin**, ELAC, PCC, CA; **Fernanda Ortiz**, Center for English as a Second Language at the University of Arizona, AZ; **Rhony Ory**, Ygnacio Valley High School, CA; **Paul Parent**, Montgomery College, MD; **Dr. Sumeeta Patnaik**, Marshall University, WV; **Oscar Pedroso**, Miami Dade College, FL; **Robin Persiani**, Sierra College, CA; **Patricia Prenz-Belkin**, Hostos Community College, NY; **Suzanne Powell**, University of Louisville, KY; **Jim Ranalli**, Iowa State University, IA; **Toni R. Randall**, Santa Monica College, CA; **Vidya Rangachari**, Mission College, CA; **Elizabeth Rasmussen**, Northern Virginia Community College, VA; **Lara Ravitch**, Truman College, IL;

**Deborah Repasz**, San Jacinto College, TX; **Marisa Recinos**, English Language Center, Brigham Young University, UT; **Andrey Reznikov**, Black Hills State University, SD; **Alison Rice**, Hunter College, NY; **Jennifer Robles**, Ventura Unified School District, CA; **Priscilla Rocha**, Clark County School District, NV; **Dzidra Rodins**, DePaul University, IL; **Maria Rodriguez**, Central High School, AZ; **Josh Rosenberger**, English Language Institute University of Montana, MT; **Alice Rosso**, Bucks County Community College, PA; **Rita Rozzi**, Xavier University, OH; **Maria Ruiz**, Victor Valley College, CA; **Kimberly Russell**, Clark College, WA; **Stacy Sabraw**, Michigan State University, MI; **Irene Sakk**, Northwestern University, IL; **Deborah Sandstrom**, University of Illinois at Chicago, IL; **Jenni Santamaria**, ABC Adult, CA; **Shaeley Santiago**, Ames High School, IA; **Peg Sarosy**, San Francisco State University, CA; **Alice Savage**, North Harris College, TX; **Donna Schaeffer**, University of Washington, WA; **Karen Marsh Schaeffer**, University of Utah, UT; **Carol Schinger**, Northern Virginia Community College, VA; **Robert Scott**, Kansas State University, KS; **Suell Scott**, Sheridan Technical Center, FL; **Shira Seaman**, Global English Academy, NY; **Richard Seltzer**, Glendale Community College, CA; **Harlan Sexton**, CUNY Queensborough Community College, NY; **Kathy Sherak**, San Francisco State University, CA; **German Silva**, Miami Dade College, FL; **Ray Smith**, Maryland English Institute, University of Maryland, MD; **Shira Smith**, NICE Program University of Hawaii, HI; **Tara Smith**, Felician College, NJ; **Monica Snow**, California State University, Fullerton, CA; **Elaine Soffer**, Nassau County Community College, NY; **Andrea Spector**, Santa Monica Community College, CA; **Jacqueline Sport**, LBWCC Luverne Center, AL; **Karen Stanely**, Central Piedmont Community College, NC; **Susan Stern**, Irvine Valley College, CA; **Ayse Stromsdorfer**, Soldan I.S.H.S., MO; **Yilin Sun**, South Seattle Community College, WA; **Thomas Swietlik**, Intrax International Institute, IL; **Nicholas Taggert**, University of Dayton, OH; **Judith Tanka**, UCLA Extension–American Language Center, CA; **Amy Taylor**, The University of Alabama Tuscaloosa, AL; **Andrea Taylor**, San Francisco State, CA; **Priscilla Taylor**, University of Southern California, CA; **Ilene Teixeira**, Fairfax County Public Schools, VA; **Shirl H. Terrell**, Collin College, TX; **Marya Teutsch-Dwyer**, St. Cloud State University, MN; **Stephen Thergesen**, ELS Language Centers, CO; **Christine Tierney**, Houston Community College, TX; **Arlene Turini**, North Moore High School, NC; **Cara Tuzzolino**, Nassau County Community College, NY; **Suzanne Van Der Valk**, Iowa State University, IA; **Nathan D. Vasarhely**, Ygnacio Valley High School, CA; **Naomi S. Verratti**, Howard Community College, MD; **Hollyahna Vettori**, Santa Rosa Junior College, CA; **Julie Vorholt**, Lewis & Clark College, OR; **Danielle Wagner**, FLS International Marymount College, CA; **Lynn Walker**, Coastline College, CA; **Laura Walsh**, City College of San Francisco, CA; **Andrew J. Watson**, The English Bakery; **Donald Weasenforth**, Collin College, TX; **Juliane Widner**, Sheepshead Bay High School, NY; **Lynne Wilkins**, Mills College, CA; **Pamela Williams**, Ventura College, CA; **Jeff Wilson**, Irvine Valley College, CA; **James Wilson**, Consomnes River College, CA; **Katie Windahl**, Cuyahoga Community College, OH; **Dolores "Lorrie" Winter**, California State University at Fullerton, CA; **Jody Yamamoto**, Kapi'olani Community College, HI; **Ellen L. Yaniv**, Boston University, MA; **Norman Yoshida**, Lewis & Clark College, OR; **Joanna Zadra**, American River College, CA; **Florence Zysman**, Santiago Canyon College, CA;

**CANADA** **Patricia Birch**, Brandon University, MB; **Jolanta Caputa**, College of New Caledonia, BC; **Katherine Coburn**, UBC's ELI, BC; **Erin Harris-Macleod**, St. Mary's University, NS; **Tami Moffatt**, English Language Institute, BC; **Kim Papple**, Brock University, ON; **Robin Peace**, Confederation College, BC;

**ASIA** **Rabiatu Abubakar**, Eton Language Centre, Malaysia; **Wiwik Andreani**, Bina Nusantara University, Indonesia; **Frank Bailey**, Baiko Gakuin University, Japan; **Mike Baker**, Kosei Junior High School, Japan; **Leonard Barrow**, Kanto Junior College, Japan; **Herman Bartelen**, Japan; **Siren Betty**, Fooyin University, Kaohsiung; **Thomas E. Bieri**, Nagoya College, Japan; **Natalie Brezden**, Global English House, Japan; **MK Brooks**, Mukogawa Women's University, Japan; **Truong Ngoc Buu**, The Youth Language School, Vietnam; **Charles Cabell**, Toyo University, Japan; **Fred Carruth**, Matsumoto University, Japan; **Frances Causer**, Seijo University, Japan; **Jeffrey Chalk**, SNU, South Korea; **Deborah Chang**, Wenzao Ursuline College of Languages, Kaohsiung; **David Chatham**, Ritsumeikan University, Japan; **Andrew Chih Hong Chen**, National Sun Yat-sen University, Kaohsiung; **Christina Chen**, Yu-Tsai Bilingual Elementary School, Taipei; **Hui-chen Chen**, Shi-Lin High School of Commerce, Taipei; **Seungmoon Choe**, K2M Language Institute, South Korea; **Jason Jeffree Cole**, Coto College, Japan; **Le Minh Cong**, Vungtau Tourism Vocational College, Vietnam; **Todd Cooper**, Toyama National College of Technology, Japan; **Marie Cosgrove**, Daito Bunka University, Japan; **Randall Cotten**, Gifu City Women's College, Japan; **Tony Cripps**, Ritsumeikan University, Japan; **Andy Cubalit**, CHS, Thailand; **Daniel Cussen**, Takushoku University, Japan; **Le Dan**, Ho Chi Minh City Electric Power College, Vietnam; **Simon Daykin**, Banghwa-dong Community Centre, South Korea; **Aimee Denham**, ILA, Vietnam; **Bryan Dickson**, David's English Center, Taipei; **Nathan Ducker**, Japan University, Japan; **Ian Duncan**, Simul International Corporate Training, Japan; **Nguyen Thi Kieu Dung**, Thang Long University, Vietnam; **Truong Quang Dung**, Tien Giang University, Vietnam; **Nguyen Thi Thuy Duong**, Vietnamese American Vocational Training College, Vietnam; **Wong Tuck Ee**, Raja Tun Azlan Science Secondary School, Malaysia; **Emilia Effendy**, International Islamic University Malaysia, Malaysia; **Bettizza Escueta**, KMUTT, Thailand; **Robert Eva**, Kaisei Girls High School, Japan; **Jim George**, Luna International Language School, Japan; **Jurgen Germeys**, Silk Road Language Center, South Korea; **Wong Ai Gnoh**, SMJK Chung Hwa Confucian, Malaysia; **Sarah Go**, Seoul Women's University, South Korea; **Peter Goosselink**, Hokkai High School, Japan; **Robert Gorden**, SNU, South Korea; **Wendy M. Gough**, St. Mary College/Nunoike Gaigo Senmon Gakko, Japan; **Tim Grose**, Sapporo Gakuin University, Japan; **Pham Thu Ha**, Le Van Tam Primary School, Vietnam; **Ann-Marie Hadzima**, Taipei; **Troy Hammond**, Tokyo Gakugei University International Secondary School, Japan; **Robiatul 'Adawiah Binti Hamzah**, SMK Putrajaya Precinct 8(1), Malaysia; **Tran Thi Thuy Hang**, Ho Chi Minh City Banking University, Vietnam; **To Thi Hong Hanh**, CEFALT, Vietnam; **George Hays**, Tokyo Kokusai Daigaku, Japan; **Janis Hearn**, Hongik University, South Korea; **Chantel Hemmi**, Jochi Daigaku, Japan; **David Hindman**, Sejong University, South Korea; **Nahn Cam Hoa**, Ho Chi Minh City University of Technology, Vietnam; **Jana Holt**, Korea University, South Korea; **Jason Hollowell**, Nihon University, Japan; **F. N. (Zoe) Hsu**, National Tainan University, Yong Kang; **Kuei-ping Hsu**, National Tsing Hua University, Hsinchu City; **Wenhua Hsu**, I-Shou University, Kaohsiung; **Luu Nguyen Quoc Hung**, Cantho University, Vietnam; **Cecile Hwang**, Changwon National University, South Korea; **Ainol Haryati Ibrahim**, Universiti Malaysia Pahang, Malaysia; **Robert Jeens**, Yonsei University, South Korea; **Linda M. Joyce**, Kyushu Sangyo University, Japan; **Dr. Nisai Kaewsanchai**, English Square Kanchanaburi, Thailand; **Aniza Kamarulzaman**, Sabah Science Secondary School, Malaysia; **Ikuko Kashiwabara**, Osaka Electro-Communication University, Japan; **Gurmit Kaur**, INTI College, Malaysia; **Nick Keane**, Japan; **Ward Ketcheson**, Aomori University, Japan; **Nicholas Kemp**, Kyushu International University, Japan; **Montchatry Ketmuni**, Rajamangala University of Technology, Thailand; **Dinh Viet Khanh**, Vietnam; **Seonok Kim**, Kangsu Jongro Language School, South Korea; **Suyeon Kim**, Anyang University, South Korea; **Kelly P. Kimura**, Soka University, Japan; **Masakazu Kimura**, Katoh Gakuen Gyoshu High School, Japan; **Gregory King**, Chubu Daigaku, Japan; **Stan Kirk**, Konan University, Japan; **Donald Knight**, Nan Hua/Fu Li Junior High Schools, Hsinchu; **Kari J. Kostiainen**, Nagoya City University, Japan; **Pattri Kuanpulpol**, Silpakorn University, Thailand; **Ha Thi Lan**, Thai Binh Teacher Training College, Vietnam; **Eric Edwin Larson**, Miyazaki Prefectural Nursing University, Japan; **David Laurence**, Chubu Daigaku, Japan; **Richard S. Lavin**, Prefectural University of Kumamoto, Japan; **Shirley Leane**, Chugoku Junior College, Japan; **I-Hsiu Lee**, Yunlin; **Nari Lee**, Park Jung PLS, South Korea; **Tae Lee**, Yonsei University, South Korea; **Lys Yongsoon Lee**, Reading Town Geumcheon, South Korea; **Mallory Leece**, Sun Moon University, South Korea; **Dang Hong Lien**, Tan Lam Upper Secondary School, Vietnam; **Huang Li-Han**, Rebecca Education Institute, Taipei; **Sovannarith Lim**, Royal University of Phnom Penh, Cambodia; **Ginger Lin**, National Kaohsiung Hospitality College, Kaohsiung; **Noel Lineker**, New Zealand/Japan; **Tran Dang Khanh Linh**, Nha Trang Teachers' Training College, Vietnam; **Daphne Liu**, Buliton English School, Taipei; **S. F. Josephine Liu**, Tien-Mu Elementary School, Taipei ; **Caroline Luo**, Tunghai University, Taichung; **Jeng-Jia Luo**, Tunghai University, Taichung; **Laura MacGregor**, Gakushuin University, Japan; **Amir Madani**, Visuttharangsi School, Thailand; **Elena Maeda**, Sacred Heart Professional Training College, Japan; **Vu Thi Thanh Mai**, Hoang Gia Education Center, Vietnam; **Kimura Masakazu**, Kato Gakuen Gyoshu High School, Japan; **Susumu Matsuhashi**, Net Link English School, Japan; **James McCrostie**, Daito Bunka University, Japan; **Joel McKee**, Inha University, South Korea; **Colin McKenzie**, Wachirawit Primary School, Thailand; **Terumi Miyazoe**, Tokyo Denki Daigaku, Japan; **William K. Moore**, Hiroshima Kokusai Gakuin University, Japan; **Kevin Mueller**, Tokyo Kokusai Daigaku, Japan; **Hudson Murrell**, Baiko Gakuin University, Japan; **Frances Namba**, Senri International School of Kwansei Gakuin, Japan; **Keiichi Narita**, Niigata University, Japan; **Kim Chung Nguyen**, Ho Chi Minh University of

Industry, Vietnam; **Do Thi Thanh Nhan**, Hanoi University, Vietnam; **Dale Kazuo Nishi**, Aoyama English Conversation School, Japan; **Huynh Thi Ai Nguyen**, Vietnam; **Dongshin Oh**, YBM PLS, South Korea; **Keiko Okada**, Dokkyo Daigaku, Japan; **Louise Ohashi**, Shukutoku University, Japan; **Yongjun Park**, Sangji University, South Korea; **Donald Patnaude**, Ajarn Donald's English Language Services, Thailand; **Virginia Peng**, Ritsumeikan University, Japan; **Suangkanok Piboonthamnont**, Rajamangala University of Technology, Thailand; **Simon Pitcher**, Business English Teaching Services, Japan; **John C. Probert**, New Education Worldwide, Thailand; **Do Thi Hoa Quyen**, Ton Duc Thang University, Vietnam; **John P. Racine**, Dokkyo University, Japan; **Kevin Ramsden**, Kyoto University of Foreign Studies, Japan; **Luis Rappaport**, Cung Thieu Nha Ha Noi, Vietnam; **Lisa Reshad**, Konan Daigaku Hyogo, Japan; **Peter Riley**, Taisho University, Japan; **Thomas N. Robb**, Kyoto Sangyo University, Japan; **Rory Rosszell**, Meiji Daigaku, Japan; **Maria Feti Rosyani**, Universitas Kristen Indonesia, Indonesia; **Greg Rouault**, Konan University, Japan; **Chris Ruddenklau**, Kindai University, Japan; **Hans-Gustav Schwartz**, Thailand; **Mary-Jane Scott**, Soongsil University, South Korea; **Dara Sheahan**, Seoul National University, South Korea; **James Sherlock**, A.P.W. Angthong, Thailand; **Prof. Shieh**, Minghsin University of Science & Technology, Xinfeng; **Yuko Shimizu**, Ritsumeikan University, Japan; **Suzila Mohd Shukor**, Universiti Sains Malaysia, Malaysia; **Stephen E. Smith**, Mahidol University, Thailand; **Moon-young Son**, South Korea; **Seunghee Son**, Anyang University, South Korea; **Mi-young Song**, Kyungwon University, South Korea; **Lisa Sood**, VUS, BIS, Vietnam; **Jason Stewart**, Taejon International Language School, South Korea; **Brian A. Stokes**, Korea University, South Korea; **Mulder Su**, Shih-Chien University, Kaohsiung; **Yoomi Suh**, English Plus, South Korea; **Yun-Fang Sun**, Wenzao Ursuline College of Languages, Kaohsiung; **Richard Swingle**, Kansai Gaidai University, Japan; **Sanford Taborn**, Kinjo Gakuin Daigaku, Japan; **Mamoru Takahashi**, Akita Prefectural University, Japan; **Tran Hoang Tan**, School of International Training, Vietnam; **Takako Tanaka**, Doshisha University, Japan; **Jeffrey Taschner**, American University Alumni Language Center, Thailand; **Matthew Taylor**, Kinjo Gakuin Daigaku, Japan; **Michael Taylor**, International Pioneers School, Thailand; **Kampanart Thammaphati**, Wattana Wittaya Academy, Thailand; **Tran Duong The**, Sao Mai Language Center, Vietnam; **Tran Dinh Tho**, Duc Tri Secondary School, Vietnam; **Huynh Thi Anh Thu**, Nhatrang College of Culture Arts and Tourism, Vietnam; **Peter Timmins**, Peter's English School, Japan; **Fumie Togano**, Hosei Daini High School, Japan; **F. Sigmund Topor**, Keio University Language School, Japan; **Tu Trieu**, Rise VN, Vietnam; **Yen-Cheng Tseng**, Chang-Jung Christian University, Tainan; **Pei-Hsuan Tu**, National Cheng Kung University, Tainan City; **Hajime Uematsu**, Hirosaki University, Japan; **Rachel Um**, Mok-dong Oedae English School, South Korea; **David Underhill**, EEExpress, Japan; **Ben Underwood**, Kugenuma High School, Japan; **Siriluck Usaha**, Sripatum University, Thailand; **Tyas Budi Utami**, Indonesia; **Nguyen Thi Van**, Far East International School, Vietnam; **Stephan Van Eycken**, Kosei Gakuen Girls High School, Japan; **Zisa Velasquez**, Taihu International School/Semarang International School, China/Indonesia; **Jeffery Walter**, Sangji University, South Korea; **Bill White**, Kinki University, Japan; **Yohanes De Deo Widyastoko**, Xaverius Senior High School, Indonesia; **Dylan Williams**, SNU, South Korea; **Jisuk Woo**, Ichean University, South Korea; **Greg Chung-Hsien Wu**, Providence University, Taichung; **Xun Xiaoming**, BLCU, China; **Hui-Lien Yeh**, Chai Nan University of Pharmacy and Science, Tainan; **Sittiporn Yodnil**, Huachiew Chalermprakiet University, Thailand; **Shamshul Helmy Zambahari**, Universiti Teknologi Malaysia, Malaysia; **Ming-Yuli**, Chang Jung Christian University, Tainan; **Aimin Fadhlee bin Mahmud Zuhodi**, Kuala Terengganu Science School, Malaysia;

**TURKEY** **Shirley F. Akis**, American Culture Association/Fomara; **Gül Akkoç**, Boğaziçi University; **Seval Akmeşe**, Haliç University; **Ayşenur Akyol**, Ege University; **Ayşe Umut Aribaş**, Beykent University; **Gökhan Asan**, Kapadokya Vocational College; **Hakan Asan**, Kapadokya Vocational College; **Julia Asan**, Kapadokya Vocational College; **Azarvan Atac**, Piri Reis University; **Nur Babat**, Kapadokya Vocational College; **Feyza Balakbabalar**, Kadir Has University; **Gözde Balikçi**, Beykent University; **Deniz Balım**, Haliç University; **Asli Başdoğan**, Kadir Has University; **Ayla Bayram**, Kapadokya Vocational College; **Pinar Bilgiç**, Kadir Has University; **Kenan Bozkurt**, Kapadokya Vocational College; **Yonca Bozkurt**, Ege University; **Frank Carr**, Piri Reis; **Mengü Noyan Çengel**, Ege University; **Elif Doğan**, Ege University; **Natalia Donmez**, 29 Mayis Üniversite; **Nalan Emirsoy**, Kadir Has University; **Ayşe Engin**, Kadir Has University; **Ayhan Gedikbaş**, Ege University; **Gülşah Gençer**, Beykent University; **Seyit Ömer Gök**, Gediz University; **Tuğba Gök**, Gediz University; **İlkay Gökçe**, Ege University; **Zeynep Birinci Guler**, Maltepe University; **Neslihan Güler**, Kadir Has University; **Sircan Gümüş**, Kadir Has University; **Nesrin Gündoğu**, T.C. Piri Reis University; **Tanju Gurpinar**, Piri Reis University; **Selin Gurturk**, Piri Reis University; **Neslihan Gurutku**, Piri Reis University; **Roger Hewitt**, Maltepe University; **Nilüfer İbrahimoğlu**, Beykent University; **Nevin Kaftelen**, Kadir Has University; **Sultan Kalin**, Kapadokya Vocational College; **Sema Kaplan Karabina**, Anadolu University; **Eray Kara**, Giresun University; **Beylü Karayazgan**, Ege University; **Darren Kelso**, Piri Reis University; **Trudy Kittle**, Kapadokya Vocational College; **Şaziye Konaç**, Kadir Has University; **Güneş Korkmaz**, Kapadokya Vocational College; **Robert Ledbury**, Izmir University of Economics; **Ashley Lucas**, Maltepe University; **Bülent Nedium Uça**, Dogus University; **Murat Nurlu**, Ege University; **Mollie Owens**, Kadir Has University; **Oya Özağaç**, Boğaziçi University; **Funda Özcan**, Ege University; **İlkay Özdemir**, Ege University; **Ülkü Öztürk**, Gediz University; **Cassondra Puls**, Anadolu University; **Yelda Sarikaya**, Cappadocia Vocational College; **Müge Şekercioğlu**, Ege University; **Melis Senol**, Canakkale Onsekiz Mart University, The School of Foreign Languages; **Patricia Sümer**, Kadir Has University; **Rex Surface**, Beykent University; **Mustafa Torun**, Kapadokya Vocational College; **Tansel Üstünloğlu**, Ege University; **Fatih Yücel**, Beykent University; **Şule Yüksel**, Ege University;

**THE MIDDLE EAST** **Amina Saif Mohammed Al Hashamia**, Nizwa College of Applied Sciences, Oman; **Jennifer Baran**, Kuwait University, Kuwait; **Phillip Chappells**, GEMS Modern Academy, U.A.E.; **Sharon Ruth Devaneson**, Ibri College of Technology, Oman; **Hanaa El-Deeb**, Canadian International College, Egypt; **Yvonne Eaton**, Community College of Qatar, Qatar; **Brian Gay**, Sultan Qaboos University, Oman; **Gail Al Hafidh**, Sharjah Women's College (HCT), U.A.E.; **Jonathan Hastings**, American Language Center, Jordan; **Laurie Susan Hilu**, English Language Centre, University of Bahrain, Bahrain; **Abraham Irannezhad**, Mehre Aval, Iran; **Kevin Kempe**, CNA-Q, Qatar; **Jill Newby James**, University of Nizwa; **Mary Kay Klein**, American University of Sharjah, U.A.E.; **Sian Khoury**, Fujairah Women's College (HCT), U.A.E.; **Hussein Dehghan Manshadi**, Farhang Pajooh & Jaam-e-Jam Language School, Iran; **Jessica March**, American University of Sharjah, U.A.E.; **Neil McBeath**, Sultan Qaboos University, Oman; **Sandy McDonagh**, Abu Dhabi Men's College (HCT), U.A.E.; **Rob Miles**, Sharjah Women's College (HCT), U.A.E.; **Michael Kevin Neumann**, Al Ain Men's College (HCT), U.A.E.;

**LATIN AMERICA** **Aldana Aguirre**, Argentina; **Claudia Almeida**, Coordenação de Idiomas, Brazil; **Cláudia Arias**, Brazil; **Maria de los Angeles Barba**, FES Acatlan UNAM, Mexico; **Lilia Barrios**, Universidad Autónoma de Tamaulipas, Mexico; **Adán Beristain**, UAEM, Mexico; **Ricardo Böck**, Manoel Ribas, Brazil; **Edson Braga**, CNA, Brazil; **Marli Buttelli**, Mater et Magistra, Brazil; **Alessandra Campos**, Inova Centro de Linguas, Brazil; **Priscila Catta Preta Ribeiro**, Brazil; **Gustavo Cestari**, Access International School, Brazil; **Walter D'Alessandro**, Virginia Language Center, Brazil; **Lilian De Gennaro**, Argentina; **Mônica De Stefani**, Quality Centro de Idiomas, Brazil; **Julio Alejandro Flores**, BUAP, Mexico; **Mirian Freire**, CNA Vila Guilherme, Brazil; **Francisco Garcia**, Colegio Lestonnac de San Angel, Mexico; **Miriam Giovanardi**, Brazil; **Darlene Gonzalez Miy**, ITESM CCV, Mexico; **Maria Laura Grimaldi**, Argentina; **Luz Dary Guzmán**, IMPAHU, Colombia; **Carmen Koppe**, Brazil; **Monica Krutzler**, Brazil; **Marcus Murilo Lacerda**, Seven Idiomas, Brazil; **Nancy Lake**, CEL-LEP, Brazil; **Cris Lazzerini**, Brazil; **Sandra Luna**, Argentina; **Ricardo Luvisan**, Brazil; **Jorge Murilo Menezes**, ACBEU, Brazil; **Monica Navarro**, Instituto Cultural A. C., Mexico; **Joacyr Oliveira**, Faculdades Metropolitanas Unidas and Summit School for Teachers, Brazil; **Ayrton Cesar Oliveira de Araujo**, E&A English Classes, Brazil; **Ana Laura Oriente**, Seven Idiomas, Brazil; **Adelia Peña Clavel**, CELE UNAM, Mexico; **Beatriz Pereira**, Summit School, Brazil; **Miguel Perez**, Instituto Cultural, Mexico; **Cristiane Perone**, Associação Cultura Inglesa, Brazil; **Pamela Claudia Pogré**, Colegio Integral Caballito / Universidad de Flores, Argentina; **Dalva Prates**, Brazil; **Marianne Rampaso**, Iowa Idiomas, Brazil; **Daniela Rutolo**, Instituto Superior Cultural Británico, Argentina; **Maione Sampaio**, Maione Carrijo Consultoria em Inglês Ltda, Brazil; **Elaine Santesso**, TS Escola de Idiomas, Brazil; **Camila Francisco Santos**, UNS Idiomas, Brazil; **Lucia Silva**, Cooplem Idiomas, Brazil; **Maria Adela Sorzio**, Instituto Superior Santa Cecilia, Argentina; **Elcio Souza**, Unibero, Brazil; **Willie Thomas**, Rainbow Idiomas, Brazil; **Sandra Villegas**, Instituto Humberto de Paolis, Argentina; **John Whelan**, La Universidad Nacional Autonoma de Mexico, Mexico

# CONTENTS

**How to Register for iQ ONLINE** ... i

## UNIT 1 Architecture 2

**Q: What are current trends in architecture?**

**Unit Video: Frank Gehry** ... 3
Note-taking Skill: Identifying key words ... 5
**Listening 1: Modern Architecture** ... 6
Listening Skill: Listening for main ideas ... 9
**Listening 2: Sustainable Architecture** ... 10
Vocabulary Skill: Collocations: nouns and verbs ... 14
Grammar: The present continuous ... 16
Pronunciation: Interjections and intonation ... 17
Speaking Skill: Drawing attention to main ideas ... 18
**Unit Assignment: Role-play a news conference** ... 20

## UNIT 2 Psychology 24

**Q: How can colors be useful?**

Note-taking Skill: Using visual elements ... 27
**Listening 1: The Colors of Nature** ... 28
Listening Skill: Understanding cause and effect ... 32
**Listening 2: Building with Color** ... 33
**Unit Video: Color Branding** ... 37
Vocabulary Skill: Word families: nouns and verbs ... 37
Grammar: *There's* and *it's* ... 39
Pronunciation: Schwa /ə/ in unstressed syllables ... 40
Speaking Skill: Asking for and giving examples ... 41
**Unit Assignment: Present a building design** ... 42

## UNIT 3 Behavioral Science 46

**Q: Why are good manners important?**

**Unit Video: Making Small Talk** ... 47
**Listening 1: Be Polite** ... 49
Listening Skill: Predicting ... 50
Note-taking Skill: Organizing notes ... 54
**Listening 2: Classroom Etiquette** ... 55
Vocabulary Skill: Synonyms ... 59
Grammar: Modal verbs *should* and *shouldn't* ... 61
Pronunciation: Final /s/ or /z/ sounds ... 62
Speaking Skill: Giving advice and making recommendations ... 63
**Unit Assignment: Give a presentation on manners** ... 64

## UNIT 4 Game Studies 68

**Q: How can games compare to real life?**

Note-taking Skill: Reviewing and editing notes ... 71
**Listening 1: Crossword Puzzles** ... 72
Listening Skill: Listening for names and dates ... 76
**Listening 2: Business Is a Game** ... 77
**Unit Video: Kids Learn about Finance** ... 81
Vocabulary Skill: Word families: suffixes ... 82
Grammar: Imperative verbs ... 83
Pronunciation: Word stress ... 84
Speaking Skill: Giving instructions ... 85
**Unit Assignment: Develop a board game** ... 86

**Audio Track List** ... B-1
**Authors and Consultants** ... B-2

# UNIT 1

Architecture

| | |
|---|---|
| **NOTE TAKING** | identifying key words |
| **LISTENING** | listening for main ideas |
| **VOCABULARY** | collocations: nouns and verbs |
| **GRAMMAR** | the present continuous |
| **PRONUNCIATION** | interjections and intonation |
| **SPEAKING** | drawing attention to main ideas |

UNIT QUESTION

# What are current trends in architecture?

**A Discuss these questions with your classmates.**

1. Think about a city you know well. Which buildings are the most attractive? The most unattractive?
2. How important is it for a city to have beautiful architecture?
3. Look at the photo. What kind of building is it? What do you think of the building?

**UNIT OBJECTIVE**  **Listen to a conversation and a class discussion. Gather information and ideas to role-play a news conference about a new office building.**

**B** **Listen to *The Q Classroom* online. Then answer these questions.**

1. How does Sophy describe modern architecture? What is her opinion of it?
2. Does Marcus agree with her? Why or why not?

iQ ONLINE **C** **Go online to watch the video about architect Frank Gehry and the museum he designed for the city of Bilbao in Spain. Then check your comprehension.**

**VIDEO VOCABULARY**

**basket case** *(n.)* someone who is extremely nervous or stressed

**evolution** *(n.)* the process of change and development over time

**innovative** *(adj.)* describing something new that uses new ways of thinking

**masterpiece** *(n.)* an artist's best piece of work

**miracle** *(n.)* something wonderful and impossible to explain

**self-conscious** *(adj.)* worried about what other people will think about you

**D** **Go to the Online Discussion Board to discuss the Unit Question with your classmates.**

**E** **Circle the statement (*a* or *b*) that you agree with the most. Then compare your answers with a partner.**

1. a. Buildings should be sustainable and energy-efficient.
   b. Buildings should be beautiful.
2. a. The buildings in a city should have a similar style.
   b. The buildings in a city should be very different from one another.
3. a. I prefer traditional architecture from 100 years ago or more.
   b. I like modern architecture.
4. a. I pay lots of attention to the architecture in my city.
   b. I never notice the architecture of the buildings around me.
5. a. Working in architecture is an interesting career.
   b. Working in architecture is not an interesting career.

**F** **Do you notice the architecture around you? Do this activity to find out.**

1. Think about a building in your city or a famous building most people know about. What does it look like? Complete the chart. Include as much information as you can.

| **Name of building:** | |
|---|---|
| **Features of building:** | **Description:** |
| **Shape:** tall? rectangular? curved? | |
| **Style:** modern? traditional? | |
| **Materials:** brick? steel? concrete? | |
| **Function:** office building? apartment building? school? home? | |
| **Other:** | |

2. Work with a partner. Describe the building to your partner. Use the information in the chart. Have your partner guess which building you described.
3. Listen to your partner describe a building. Which building is your partner describing?

## Note-taking Skill | Identifying key words

When you take notes, write only *key* words—the most important words. Don't spend time writing little words like *of, the, and,* etc. These are some ways to identify key words as you listen:

- Listen for repeated words. These often point to the main idea.
- Focus on words that the speaker defines. If a speaker takes time to say what a word means, it's probably important.
- Listen for words the speaker emphasizes by saying them more slowly or a little louder.

**A. Read the paragraph that introduces a podcast titled "Careers in Architecture." Underline the most important words. The words *career opportunities* are underlined as an example.**

You may not be aware of it, but there are a variety of career opportunities in the field of architecture. Being an architect is, of course, the first one everyone thinks of, but there are many others. So if you are creative and have a good visual imagination, consider one of these careers.

**B. Listen as the speaker describes three different careers in architecture. Write the important words. Does the speaker repeat any of the words you underlined in Activity A?**

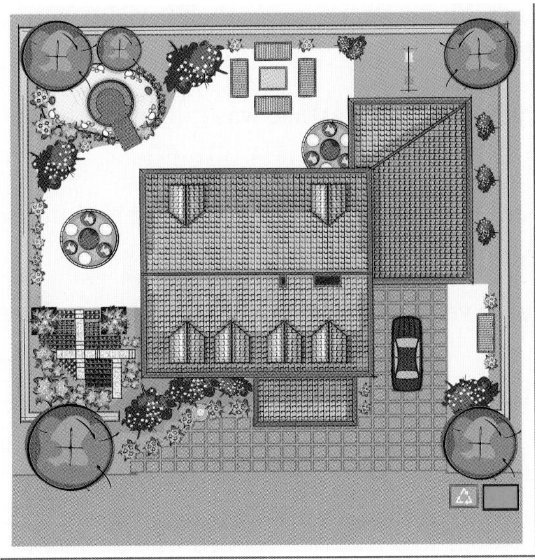

A landscape architect's plan

**C. Compare notes with a partner. Which words did you write? Why?**

**D. Go online for more practice with identifying key words.**

# LISTENING

## LISTENING 1 | Modern Architecture

**You are going to listen to a conversation between two newspaper journalists, Vicky and Julia. Vicky has to write a story about architect Oscar Valerian's design for the city's new library. As you listen to the conversation, gather information and ideas about the current trends in architecture.**

### PREVIEW THE LISTENING

**A. VOCABULARY Here are some words from Listening 1. Read the sentences. Then match each underlined word with its definition below.**

_d_ 1. Energy-efficient houses are a new architectural trend. Many people want them now.

___ 2. Five years ago, no one knew who he was. Now he's a celebrity. His name is in the newspaper every day.

___ 3. That's the most ridiculous idea I've ever heard. It will never work.

___ 4. Bill told a joke at dinner last night. We all laughed very hard.

___ 5. Driving a car without wearing a seatbelt is risky. You can get hurt in an accident.

___ 6. The person who wrote the article was critical of the book. He didn't like it at all.

___ 7. He's an experienced journalist. He works for an important newspaper company.

___ 8. I admire Elaine very much. She's a great author and a very nice person.

a. (*verb*) to respect someone very much
b. (*noun*) a famous person
c. (*adjective*) saying that something is bad or wrong
d. (*noun*) a popular idea or change
e. (*noun*) a thing that someone says that is funny, not serious
f. (*noun*) a person who collects, writes, and publishes news
g. (*adjective*) very silly or unreasonable
h. (*adjective*) dangerous



Oxford 3000™ words

**B.** Go online for more practice with the vocabulary.

**C.** PREVIEW You are going to listen to a conversation between Vicky and Julia about an architectural design. Work with a partner. What key words do you think you will hear in the conversation? Make a list.

## WORK WITH THE LISTENING

**A.** LISTEN AND TAKE NOTES Listen to the conversation. Write the key words you hear. Leave space on the page to add more notes later. Here are some words to help you get started.

*the new city library*

*architect*

*plan = ridiculous?*

**B.** Listen again. Add more information to your notes.

**C.** Check (✓) the two statements that express main ideas in the conversation.

____ 1. Julia is writing an article about the president's speech.

____ 2. Vicky thinks that there are some serious problems with the plans for the new library.

____ 3. The mayor and members of the city council were at the meeting.

____ 4. People are sometimes afraid to criticize a new style or trend because of what other people may think.

**D.** Answer the questions. Then listen and check your answers.

1. What does Vicky say the new library design looks like?

___________________________________________

2. How many people were at the meeting?

___________________________________________

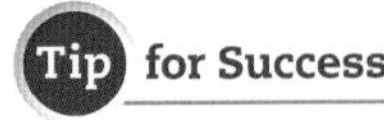

Many students are nervous about listening. Relax! If you are nervous or stressed, it's more difficult to listen and understand what you hear.

3. Did people laugh when they saw the plans?

_______________________________________________

4. What does Vicky think about the architect's plans?

_______________________________________________

5. What do people in the town think of Oscar Valerian's work?

_______________________________________________

6. Why does Vicky feel that it is important to be critical of the library design?

_______________________________________________

7. What advice does Julia give Vicky about her article?

_______________________________________________

8. Will Vicky follow Julia's advice? What do you think?

_______________________________________________

**E. Who said it? Mark each statement as *J* (Julia) or *V* (Vicky).**

____ 1. I can take a break. What's up?

____ 2. I don't know what to say.

____ 3. You're joking.

____ 4. I thought it was a joke, but it wasn't.

____ 5. We need a bigger building with lots of room for books and computers.

____ 6. This architect is sort of a celebrity.

____ 7. For one thing, you're going to make a lot of people unhappy.

____ 8. I need to give my honest opinion of the plans for the library even if it's risky.

**F. Work with a partner. Continue Julia and Vicky's conversation. Follow these guidelines. Then present your conversation to the class.**

Julia: Give Vicky three suggestions for things she can say in her article. After each suggestion, give Vicky time to answer.

Vicky: Agree or disagree with each of Julia's suggestions. Explain why.

Example:

Julia: *You can say that the ball is a good modern design, but it doesn't look good in the neighborhood.*

Vicky: *Hmm. I don't know. That isn't really what I think. (OR That's a great idea. That doesn't sound so critical.)*

(Note: You can use your own names instead of the names Julia and Vicky.)

## SAY WHAT YOU THINK

**Discuss the questions in a group.**

**Critical Thinking Tip**

Question 1 asks you to **give examples**. Giving examples is a way to show you understand an idea.

1. Do you think that architects should follow the latest trends? Why or why not? Give examples.
2. What architectural styles do you admire? What kinds of buildings do you dislike?
3. A famous architect said, "Buildings should serve people, not the other way around." What do you think this means? Do you agree? Why or why not?

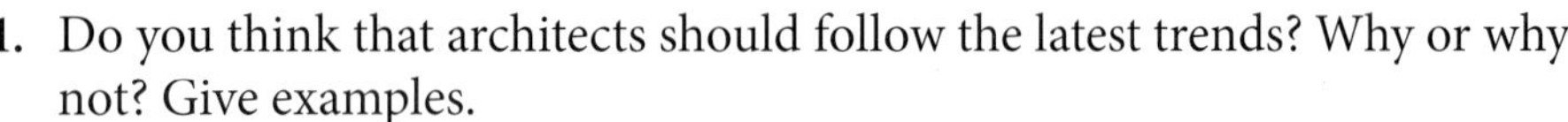

## Listening Skill | Listening for main ideas

The **main idea** is the most important thing the speaker wants you to understand. Focus on understanding the main idea first. Listen for repeated ideas. Pay attention when a speaker emphasizes a sentence. Don't stop to think about words you don't understand. Keep listening.

**A. Listen to a short presentation on trends in furniture design. Check (✓) the sentence that best states the speaker's main idea.**

____ 1. Many furniture makers these days are using recycled materials.

____ 2. Trends in furniture design in the 21st century are similar to trends in building designs.

____ 3. People sometimes feel nostalgic when they remember things they saw in their grandparents' homes.

**B. Listen again. Work with a partner. Discuss the questions.**

1. Which of these words from the Listening did you NOT understand? Circle them.

| deforestation | echoed | gadgets | impact |
|---|---|---|---|
| nostalgia | notable | stuff | vintage |

2. Why was it possible to understand the main idea without knowing these words?
3. What examples did the speaker use? How did they help you understand the main idea?

**C. Go online for more practice with listening for main ideas.**

## LISTENING 2 | Sustainable Architecture

**You are going to listen to part of a college architecture class. The instructor is leading a discussion of something called sustainable architecture. As you listen to the discussion, gather information and ideas about the current trends in architecture.**

### PREVIEW THE LISTENING

**A. VOCABULARY Here are some words from Listening 2. Read their definitions. Then complete each sentence.**

**benefit** (*noun*) 🔑 a good or useful effect of something
**combination** (*noun*) 🔑 two or more things mixed or joined together
**eco-friendly** (*adjective*) not harmful to the environment
**economics** (*noun*) 🔑 the financial element of something; how it involves money
**forest** (*noun*) 🔑 a large area of land covered with trees
**relationship** (*noun*) 🔑 a connection between two or more people
**roof** (*noun*) 🔑 the structure that covers the top of a building
**sustainable** (*adjective*) using natural materials and energy in a way that can continue without harming the environment

🔑 Oxford 3000™ words

1. They're studying the ________________ of the fashion industry. They want to know how much people spend on clothes and how this affects business in the area.

2. Look at all the water on the floor! I think there is a hole in the ________________.

3. Electric cars are more ________________ than cars that use gas.

4. Sandra and I have a good ________________. We understand each other very well.

5. One ________________ of a job with an airline company is that you can travel for free.

6. People are cutting down a lot of trees to build houses. This activity is not ________________. Soon there will be no more trees!

7. Behind our house, there is a small ________________ with a variety of trees and other plants.

8. This is a new flavor. It's like a ________________ of orange and banana. I like the way they taste together!

iQ ONLINE **B. Go online for more practice with the vocabulary.**

## WORK WITH THE LISTENING

**A. LISTEN AND TAKE NOTES Listen to the discussion. Write the key words you hear. Leave space on the page to add more notes later. Here are some words to help you get started.**

*sustainable architecture*

*relationship*

*environment*

**B.** **Listen again. Add more information to your notes.**

**C.** **Read the questions. Circle the correct answers.**

**Tip for Success**

Keep your notes very short. Write only single words or short phrases to help you remember an idea. Then complete your notes with more information.

1. What is sustainable architecture?
   a. architecture that uses traditional methods to build modern buildings
   b. architecture that tries not to harm the environment
   c. architecture that uses a lot of different materials
2. Do the students mention any economic benefits of sustainable architecture?
   a. Yes, they say it creates jobs for builders.
   b. No, they say it is a more expensive way to build.
   c. Yes, they say it saves on energy costs.
3. Which of these is NOT true of sustainable architecture?
   a. It is encouraging architects to create new and attractive building designs.
   b. It is good for the environment, but the buildings are kind of boring.
   c. Buildings can be sustainable, economical, and also beautiful at the same time.

**D.** **Read the questions. Circle the answer that best completes each statement. Then listen again and check your answers.**

1. The instructor believes that ____.
   a. it is important to build sustainably, even if it is more expensive
   b. sustainable architecture needs to be economical and good for the environment
   c. sustainable architecture has no economic benefits
2. Rafi says that solar-energy systems ____.
   a. are expensive, but they save money in electric bills
   b. are cheaper to put in than other systems
   c. will increase people's electric bills
3. Kim says that the Vertical Forest (*Bosco Verticale*) is ____.
   a. a tall apartment building with a forest around it
   b. a large public park in the middle of Milan
   c. two apartment buildings with trees on all the balconies

**The Vertical Forest (*Bosco Verticale*)**

4. The trees in the Vertical Forest ____.
   a. make the apartments hot and dark
   b. clean the air and keep the apartments cool
   c. are going to be a problem for the people in the building

5. At the end of the class, the instructor does NOT ____.
   a. give the students a test on the lecture
   b. review the important points of the discussion
   c. give the students homework for the next day

**E. Work with a partner. The graph below describes the increase in the use of green roofs in North America. Discuss the questions.**

1. How much did the use of green roofs in North America increase between 2004 and 2012?
2. When did the biggest increase occur?
3. Why do you think green roofs are becoming more popular?
4. Do you know of any buildings in your community that have a "green roof"?

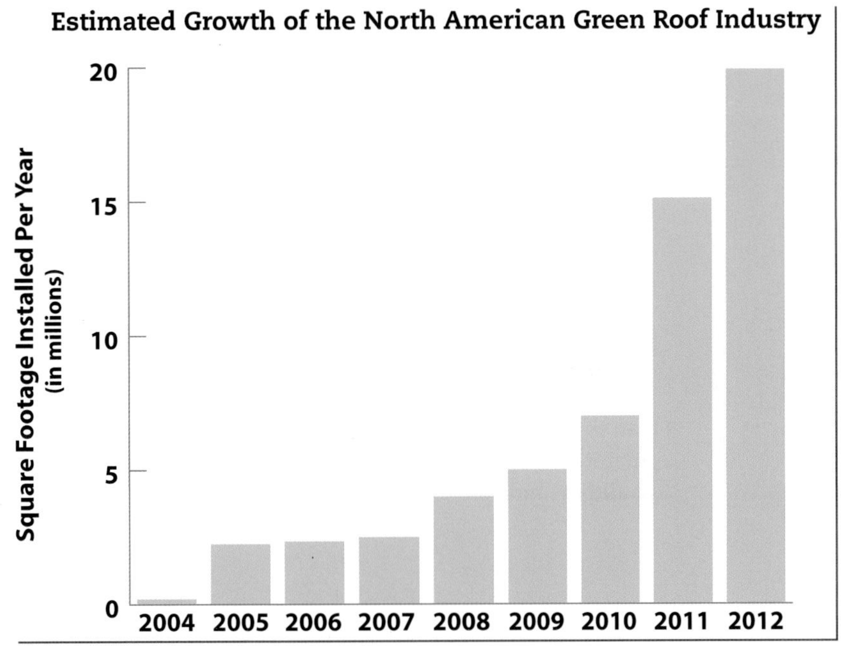


Source: Green Roofs for Healthy Cities, Annual Green Roof Industry Survey for 2012 www.greenroofs.org

**F. Go online to listen to *Burj Khalifa* and check your comprehension.**

## SAY WHAT YOU THINK

**A. Discuss the questions in a group.**

1. What are some other ways architects can design sustainable buildings and homes?
2. Is living in a sustainable home important to you? Why or why not?

**B. Think about the video, Listening 1, and Listening 2 as you discuss the questions.**

1. What are some trends in modern architecture? What different trends did Listening 1 and Listening 2 suggest?
2. How modern is the city you live in? How sustainable is the architecture?
3. Imagine a world without creative architects. What would our cities look like?

## Vocabulary Skill | Collocations: nouns and verbs

**Tip for Success**

Look at the words around a word you don't know. They can help you find the meaning of the new word.

**Collocations** are groups of words that are commonly used together. One type of collocation is the **noun** + **verb** combination.

The word web shows verbs often used with the noun *home* and with other related words.

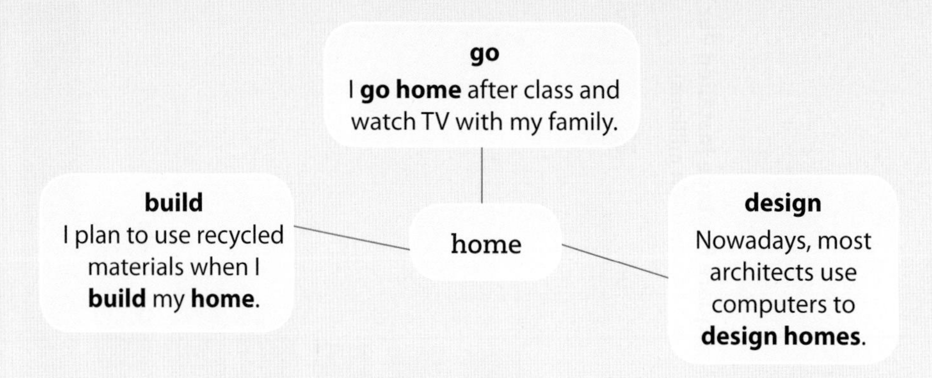

**A.** **Read the sentences. Underline the verbs used with the noun *trend*.**

1. Hey, your shoes look cool! I'm going to get some, too. We can start a trend.
2. Franco doesn't like to follow architectural trends. His buildings follow a classical style.
3. I wasn't trying to set a trend. I rode my bike to work because I missed the bus.
4. More and more people are driving cars, even for short distances. I want to stop the trend. I'm going to start walking everywhere I go.
5. Buildings in my city are getting more energy efficient. I hope architects continue this trend.

**B.** **Complete the word web. Use the words you underlined in Activity A.**

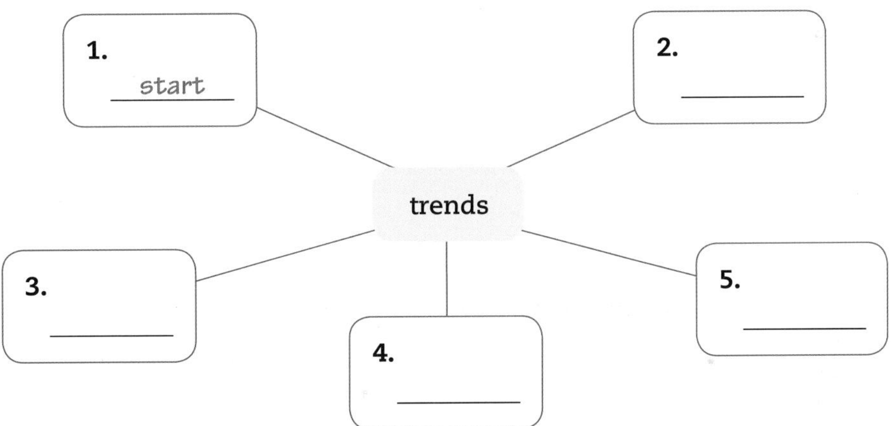


iQ ONLINE **C.** **Go online for more practice with noun and verb collocations.**

# SPEAKING

**At the end of this unit, you are going to participate in a role-play of a news conference about a new office building in your community. As you speak, you will need to highlight your main ideas.**

## Grammar The present continuous

The **present continuous** describes actions that take place at the moment of speaking.

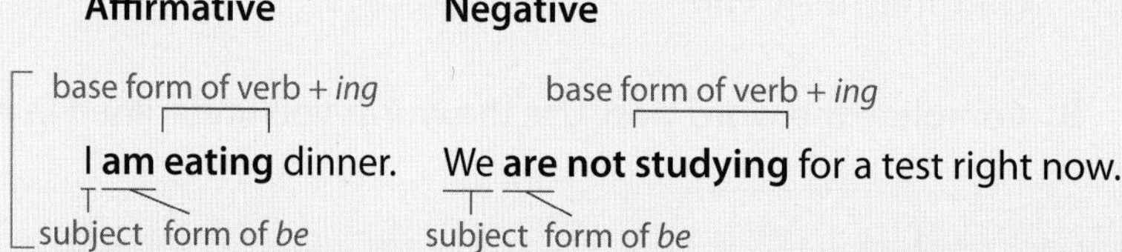


The present continuous also describes actions that take place around now, but not exactly at the moment of speaking. The actions continue for a period of time. Look for clue words and phrases like *today*, *this week*, *this year*, and *always*.

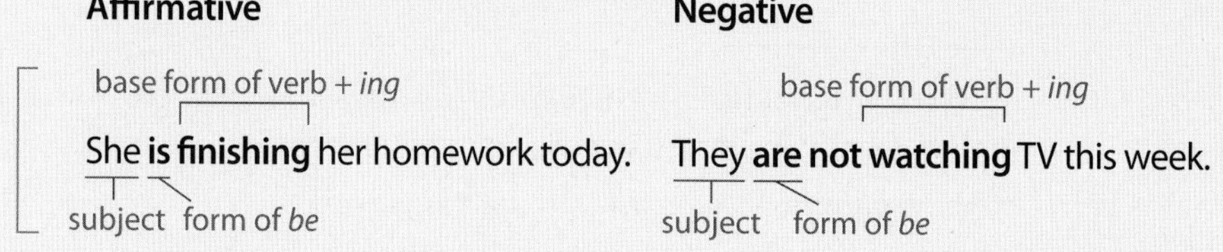


**A. Write sentences. Use the present continuous. Then read your sentences to a partner.**

1. My cousin / study / architecture at university

   *My cousin is studying architecture at university.*

2. Mark / attend / the conference on sustainability / today

   ______________________________

3. We / discuss / modern architecture / this week

   ______________________________

4. Right now / Professor Martin / talk / to some students

   ______________________________

**B.** **Listen to the conversations. Do they describe actions that are happening now or actions that are happening around now? Write *HN* (happening now) or *AN* (happening around now).**

1. ________________
2. ________________
3. ________________
4. ________________
5. ________________
6. ________________

iQ ONLINE

**C.** **Go online for more practice with the present continuous.**

**D.** **Go online for the grammar expansion.**

## Pronunciation Interjections and intonation

**Interjections** are short words, phrases, or sounds that people use when they speak. Interjections often express feelings. For example, *Wow!* is an interjection that usually indicates surprise or excitement.

> **Wow!** That dress is fantastic! I love it.

The meaning of an interjection often depends on the speaker's **intonation**. For example, *Oh!* can express different emotions, as in these examples.

> **Oh!** I didn't know you were coming. (happiness)
> **Oh!** I failed my driving test again. (disappointment)
> **Oh!** Someone parked their car right behind us. Now we can't get out. (anger)

Other common interjections are *well* and *yeah*.

**A.** **Listen to the sentences. Two different speakers will read each one. Answer the questions. Check (✓) the correct speaker.**

1. **Well,** I think this is the right answer.

   Which speaker sounds more uncertain?

   ___ Speaker 1

   ___ Speaker 2

2. **Yeah,** and after we finish this project, we're going to do another one.

   Which speaker sounds more excited?

   ___ Speaker 1

   ___ Speaker 2

3. **Yeah,** I lost my presentation.

   Which speaker sounds more disappointed?

   ___ Speaker 1

   ___ Speaker 2

4. **Oh!** Mr. Lombardi is going to be in Tokyo next week.

   Which speaker sounds happier?

   ___ Speaker 1

   ___ Speaker 2

iQ ONLINE **B. Go online for more practice with interjections and intonation.**

## Speaking Skill Drawing attention to main ideas

When you speak, help listeners understand your main ideas.

- Repeat an important idea with different words.

Buildings should serve people, not the other way around. **In other words,** architects should remember the real, practical purpose of a building as they design it.

- Use phrases for emphasis.

**The key point is** that buildings should serve people, not the other way around.

- Summarize the main ideas of the presentation.

**To sum up,** architects should consider both the form and function of a building.

**A.** **Read the lecture "Is Archictecture Art?" Underline an example of each strategy from the Speaking Skill box. Write *1*, *2*, and *3* near the underlined text.**

## Is Architecture Art?

Think for a minute about the word *architecture*. What words do you think of? Maybe you thought of building materials, styles, or different shapes and colors. How many of you thought of art?

In fact, architecture is an art. Artists use shapes and colors in their work. Artists also use different materials and work in different styles. They make drawings with pen or pencil. They paint with watercolor or oils. Some artists' work is very modern, yet others still prefer more traditional styles. People have different opinions about both works of art and architecture.

The key point is, however, that there is a difference between architecture and other art forms. People have to live and work in the buildings that architects design. We don't have to "live" in a painting. Our homes protect us from the weather. They keep us warm in the winter and dry when it rains. They protect us from other dangers on the outside—for example, other people who might want to hurt us in some way. Other buildings provide spaces for people to come together for public meetings, concerts, or sporting events. In other words, architecture is a useful art. We want the buildings we move around in every day to be beautiful, but they also have to be safe and comfortable.

To sum up, architecture is a form of art. It is creative and uses many of the same elements that artists use. People look at buildings and admire or criticize the way they look, just as they do with artwork. But a building also has to be useful and practical.

**The Scottish Parliament Building**

**B.** **Work in a group. Choose one of the following statements and talk about it to the group for one minute. Give examples and draw attention to the main ideas. Take turns.**

1. I would like to live in (an old / a very modern) house.
2. Being an architect is a creative and interesting career.
3. I think that ________________ is the most beautiful building in our community.

**C.** **Go online for more practice with drawing attention to main ideas.**

## Unit Assignment Role-play a news conference

In this section, you will play the role of either an architect or a journalist at a news conference. The architects are presenting plans for a new office building in the main business district of your city. Journalists are questioning the architects about the plans for the building. As you prepare your role-play, think about the Unit Question, "What are current trends in architecture?" Use information from Listening 1, Listening 2, the unit video, and your work in this unit to support your role-play. Refer to the Self-Assessment checklist on page 22.

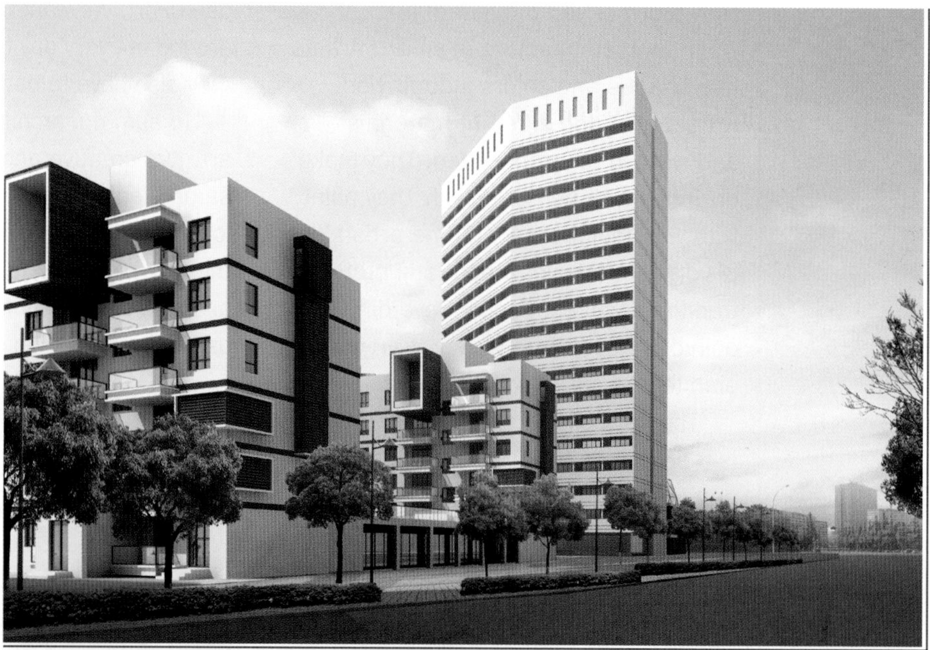

## CONSIDER THE IDEAS

**Listen as the head architect starts a news conference about the new office building. Answer the questions.**

1. Why does the city council support the building?
2. What questions are critics asking?

## PREPARE AND SPEAK

**A. GATHER IDEAS Think about the questions journalists might ask and the information the architects will need for the news conference. Make notes about these topics. Use your own ideas.**

| Topic | Notes |
|---|---|
| size of building | How tall is the building? (12 floors) |
| energy use | |
| parking | |
| location / neighborhood | |
| interior of building / uses | |
| landscaping / green roof | |

**B. ORGANIZE IDEAS Work in groups of five or six, if possible. Assign each person the role of either journalist or architect, at least two for each role.**

Journalists: Meet and prepare questions for the interview. Use your notes from Activity A to help you.

Architects: Meet and consider the questions journalists might ask. Prepare answers. Use your notes from Activity A to help you. Remember, the architects are all working on the same building. They have to agree.

**C. SPEAK Role-play the news conference. Choose one of the architects to be the leader. As you do the role-play, think about news conferences you see on TV. Refer to the Self-Assessment checklist on page 22 before you begin.**

1. During the news conference, . . .
   - journalists raise their hands to ask questions.
   - the leader calls on journalists.
   - each journalist should ask at least one question.
   - each architect should answer at least one question.
   - journalists take notes to use when they write their reports.
2. Present your role-play to the class.

**Go online for your alternate Unit Assignment.**

# CHECK AND REFLECT

**A. CHECK Think about the Unit Assignment as you complete the Self-Assessment checklist.**

| SELF-ASSESSMENT | | |
|---|---|---|
| Yes | No | |
| ☐ | ☐ | I was able to speak easily about the topic. |
| ☐ | ☐ | My partner, group, class understood me. |
| ☐ | ☐ | I used the present continuous. |
| ☐ | ☐ | I used vocabulary from the unit. |
| ☐ | ☐ | I drew attention to main ideas. |
| ☐ | ☐ | I used intonation to express feelings. |

**B. REFLECT Go to the Online Discussion Board to discuss these questions.**

1. What is something new you learned in this unit?
2. Look back at the Unit Question—What are current trends in architecture? Is your answer different now than when you started this unit? If yes, how is it different? Why?

# TRACK YOUR SUCCESS

**Circle the words you have learned in this unit.**

**Nouns**
benefit AWL
celebrity
combination
economics AWL
forest
joke
journalist
relationship
roof
trend AWL

**Verbs**
admire

**Adjectives**
critical
eco-friendly
ridiculous
risky
sustainable AWL

Oxford 3000™ words
AWL Academic Word List

**Check (✓) the skills you learned. If you need more work on a skill, refer to the page(s) in parentheses.**

| | |
|---|---|
| NOTE TAKING | ☐ I can identify key words. (p. 5) |
| LISTENING | ☐ I can listen for main ideas. (p. 9) |
| VOCABULARY | ☐ I can use noun and verb collocations. (p. 14) |
| GRAMMAR | ☐ I can use the present continuous. (p. 16) |
| PRONUNCIATION | ☐ I can use interjections and intonation. (p. 17) |
| SPEAKING | ☐ I can draw attention to main ideas. (p. 18) |
| UNIT OBJECTIVE  | ☐ I can gather information and ideas to role-play a news conference about a new office building. |

UNIT 2

Psychology

NOTE TAKING ▶ using visual elements
LISTENING ▶ understanding cause and effect
VOCABULARY ▶ word families: nouns and verbs
GRAMMAR ▶ *there's* and *it's*
PRONUNCIATION ▶ schwa /ə/ in unstressed syllables
SPEAKING ▶ asking for and giving examples

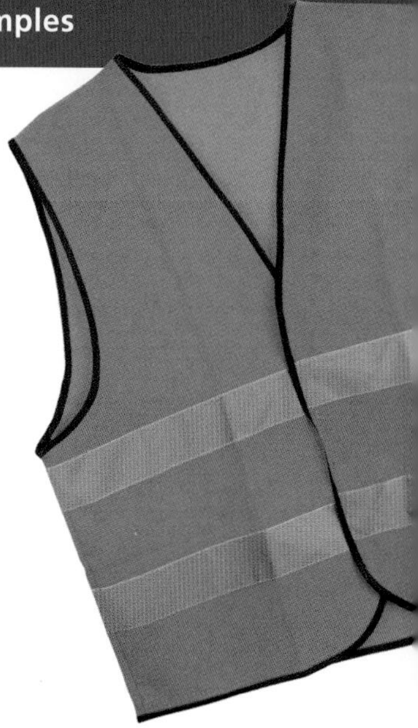

UNIT QUESTION

# How can colors be useful?

**A Discuss these questions with your classmates.**

1. Why can wearing dark clothes at night be dangerous? Why do traffic police in some countries wear orange?
2. Imagine you want to paint your house. What color do you choose? Why?
3. Look at the photo. How is color useful to this animal?

**UNIT OBJECTIVE** Listen to a nature program and a panel presentation. Gather information and ideas to give a presentation about the use of color.

**B** Listen to *The Q Classroom* online. Then match the ideas in the box to the students in the chart.

| | | |
|---|---|---|
| a. to affect moods | ~~b. for symbolic reasons~~ | c. hospitals use relaxing colors |
| d. to attract attention | e. different-colored notebooks | f. to organize |
| g. wearing school colors | h. big red letters on a sign | |

| | Use of color | Example |
|---|---|---|
| Sophy | *b. for symbolic reasons* | |
| Felix | | |
| Marcus | | |
| Yuna | | |

**C** Go to the Online Discussion Board to discuss the Unit Question with your classmates.

**D** Complete the questionnaire. Then compare answers with a partner.

## Animals Around Us

| ANIMAL | WHERE YOU SEE THEM | ANIMAL'S COLORS |
|---|---|---|
| bird | ☐ at home<br>☐ in the yard<br>☐ in the park<br>☐ other ________ | ________<br>________<br>________ |
| mouse | ☐ at home<br>☐ in the yard<br>☐ in the park<br>☐ other ________ | ________<br>________<br>________ |
| cat | ☐ at home<br>☐ in the yard<br>☐ in the park<br>☐ other ________ | ________<br>________<br>________ |

**E** **Discuss the following questions with your partner. How easy or difficult is it to see these animals? Does it have anything to do with their colors? Why or why not?**

**F** **Look at the photo. The man is wearing a special kind of clothing called *camouflage*. It has the same colors as the grass. Why is this clothing useful for his job?**

An animal photographer

## Note-taking Skill | Using visual elements

Instructors often use visual elements in their classes. They sometimes refer to pictures in a textbook or show photographs and charts on a screen. They also draw simple pictures and diagrams on the board. To use a visual element in your notes, you can . . .

- first copy the picture or diagram into your notes.
- then label the picture and write notes around it.

You don't need to be a great artist to use pictures in your notes. Even a rough drawing will help you remember the contents of the class.

**A.** **Look at the picture of a leaf used in a biology class and read the instructor's explanation. Then finish labeling the student's drawing and write notes.**

**The Structure of a Leaf**

**The Structure of a Leaf**

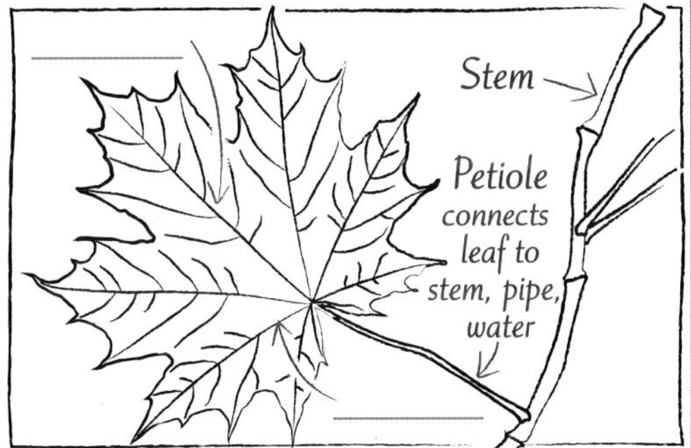


The leaves are the food-making part of a plant. The *petiole* connects the leaf to a *stem* on the plant. The petiole is like a small tube or pipe. It carries water and minerals to the leaf. Water goes from the petiole to the *midrib*. The midrib runs from the bottom to the top of the leaf. Then small *veins* distribute this water all through the leaf. The petiole also turns the leaf toward the sun. This is important because leaves use energy from the sun to make food from carbon dioxide in the air and water. This process is called *photosynthesis*.

**B.** **Look at the picture of the tree and listen as an instructor describes the parts of a tree. Copy the drawing and make notes.**

**Parts of a Tree**

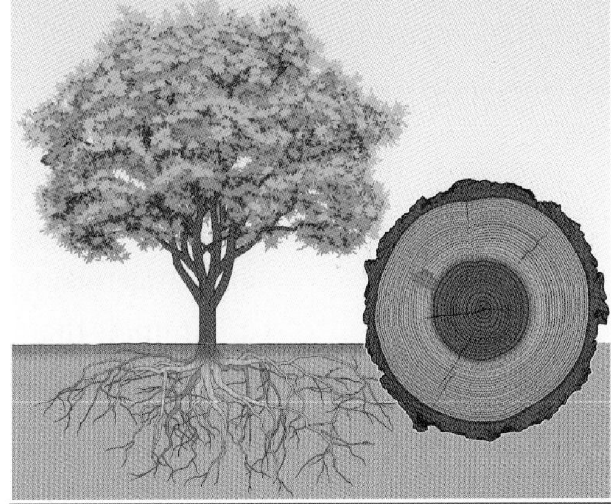

**C.** **Go online for more practice using visual elements in your notes.**

# LISTENING

## LISTENING 1 | The Colors of Nature

**You are going to listen to part of a nature program. A famous scientist talks about how animals use color. As you listen to the program, gather information and ideas about how colors can be useful.**

### PREVIEW THE LISTENING

**A. VOCABULARY Here are some words from Listening 1. Read the sentences. Then circle the answer that best matches the meaning of each underlined word.**

1. Animals hide when danger is near. They come out when it's safe.
   a. go to a place where no one can see them
   b. come out and look around
2. Listen to that bird. I think it's giving the other birds a warning that there's a cat hunting them.
   a. a call that means hunger
   b. a call that means danger
3. Don't let the children touch that. It is rat poison. It can hurt them.
   a. something that is dangerous to touch or eat
   b. something that has a very bad taste
4. This hand cream makes your skin soft and beautiful.
   a. outer covering of your body
   b. shoes and clothing
5. Some large birds have wings that are more than six feet across.
   a. body parts used to walk
   b. body parts used to fly
6. Most pets can't survive in the wild. They need people to take care of them.
   a. stay alive
   b. find friends
7. Lions are predators. Other animals stay away from lions because they are dangerous.
   a. animals that live in a group
   b. animals that kill and eat other animals
8. All insects have six legs, and many have wings. Most are very small.
   a. an animal like an ant or a bee
   b. an animal like a cat or a rabbit



Oxford 3000™ words

**B.** Go online for more practice with the vocabulary.

**C.** **PREVIEW** You are going to listen to a nature program about ways animals use color. Work with a partner. Discuss these questions.

1. Look at photos 1 and 2. Why is it difficult to see the animals in these photos?
2. Look at photo 3. Is it easy or difficult to see the frog?
3. Why do you think the animals have these colors?

1 A false-leaf katydid

2 A cryptic frog

3 A blue poison dart frog

## WORK WITH THE LISTENING

**A.** Look at the photos again. Make rough sketches of the animals on a page for your notes. Label the photos and make notes about what you see—for example, color, size, or location. Leave room on the page to add more information.

**B.** **LISTEN AND TAKE NOTES** Listen to the nature program and take more notes about each animal in the photos.

**C.** Complete the chart with the words in the box. Then listen and check your answers.

| | | |
|---|---|---|
| among the green leaves | blue | brown |
| on the forest floor | green | in the rain forest |

| | False-leaf katydid | Cryptic frog | Poison dart frog |
|---|---|---|---|
| color | | | |
| location | | | |

**D.** **Read the sentences. Then listen again. Circle the answer that best completes each statement.**

1. The false-leaf katydid's ___ look just like leaves.
   a. eyes
   b. wings
   c. legs

2. The katydid gets its name from ___.
   a. a girl named Katy
   b. the way it looks
   c. a sound it makes

3. The colors of the cryptic frog match the leaves and ___ on the forest floor.
   a. rocks
   b. insects
   c. flowers

4. The best way to see a cryptic frog is to ___.
   a. wait for the wind to blow
   b. watch for it to move
   c. look under a rock

5. The blue poison dart frog has enough poison to kill ___.
   a. one person
   b. five people
   c. ten people

6. Poison dart frogs live in the rain forests of ___.
   a. South America
   b. South Africa
   c. North America

**E.** **Work with a partner. Take turns asking and answering the questions. Use your own words.**

1. What does the word *camouflage* mean?
2. Why do animals use camouflage? Give an example from the Listening or from your own experience.
3. How does the poison dart frog use color? How is it different from the cryptic frog?

**F.** **Read the descriptions of these animals. Do you think they use color for camouflage or as a warning? Write *C* (camouflage) or *W* (warning). Compare answers with a partner.**

1

2

3

4

4

____ 1. Monarch butterflies are bright orange. Their wings have a terrible taste.

____ 2. Zebras are African animals in the horse family. They have black and white stripes. You often find them standing in tall grass.

____ 3. The coral snake lives in forests. It has red, yellow, and black stripes.

____ 4. The arctic fox has brown or gray fur in the summer, but in winter its fur changes to white.

## SAY WHAT YOU THINK

**Discuss the questions in a group.**

1. Think about the animals in Activity D on page 26. Do these animals use color for camouflage or as a warning? Explain.
2. Most large predators, like lions, are not brightly colored. Why do you think this is true?
3. What are some ways people use color as camouflage or as a sign of danger?

## Listening Skill | Understanding cause and effect

A **cause** is the action that makes something happen. An **effect** is what happens as a result. In a sentence, the cause can come before the effect or after it.

Connecting words like *so* and *because* show a cause or an effect. Listen for them carefully. *So* shows an effect. *Because* shows a cause.

Pollution was a poison to the frogs, **so** the frogs in the pond died.
cause
effect
The frogs survived **because** their camouflage matched the leaves.
effect
cause


**A. Listen to these statements about the nature program you heard in Listening 1. Circle the cause in each statement. Underline the effect.**

1. Katydids are hard to see because of their green color.
2. Predators can't see the katydids, so the katydids stay safe.
3. It's hard to see the cryptic frog because it uses camouflage.
4. The cryptic frog is the same color as the leaves, so you can't see it very well.
5. The blue poison dart frog is bright blue so you can see it easily.
6. Dart frogs are dangerous because their skins contain a strong poison.

**B. Listen to the scientist talk about Australian bowerbirds. Then match each cause with the correct effect.**

A male bowerbird and its bower

| Cause | Effect |
|---|---|
| ___ **1.** The satin bowerbird decorates its bower with blue things. | a. The bower looks nice. |
| ___ **2.** The bowerbird doesn't like red. | b. Predators cannot find the nest easily. |
| ___ **3.** The female builds a nest in a tree. | c. The bowerbird removes the red thing. |

**C. Go online for more practice with understanding cause and effect.**

# LISTENING 2 | Building with Color

**You are going to listen to a class presentation about how two different architects use color in their work. The presentation includes photographs of the architects' work. As you listen to the presentation, gather information and ideas.**

## PREVIEW THE LISTENING

**Vocabulary Skill Review**

In Unit 1, you learned about noun + verb collocations. Can you find any noun + verb collocations in the paragraph in Activity A? Underline them.

**A.** **VOCABULARY** **Here are some words from Listening 2. Read the paragraph. Then write each underlined word next to the correct definition.**

### Building My Dream House

Like most people, I have a dream home. I want to build my home in the country, not the city. I want to get away from urban life. I even drew pictures of the house. Of course I'm not a real architect, so my drawings are not perfect. I want to use natural materials in the home, like wood and stone, not blocks of concrete. I know exactly where I want to build it. The site is by a lake in the mountains. I want to paint the house brown and green to blend in with the trees around it, not stand out. I want the house to be round, not square, because a circle is a more natural shape. The high roof of the house can be gray. Gray matches the color of the rocks in the mountain. The road to the house isn't straight. It follows an old, curving walking path. Some of my friends don't like my idea. They advise me not to waste money on the house, but someday I am going to build my dream house.

1. ________________ (*phrasal verb*) to look different from the things around
2. ________________ (*phrasal verb*) to look like the things around
3. ________________ (*noun*) a hard, man-made building material
4. ________________ (*verb*) to be the same color as something else
5. ________________ (*noun*) the form of something, such as a circle or square
6. ________________ (*noun*) a place or location
7. ________________ (*adjective*) in a direct line, not curved
8. ________________ (*adjective*) related to the city, not the country
9. ________________ (*verb*) to tell someone what you think he or she should do

**B.** **Go online for more practice with the vocabulary.**

**C.** **PREVIEW** Look at the two photos from the presentation. How are the colors different? Discuss with a partner.

Great Bamboo Wall House

Hundertwasser House

## WORK WITH THE LISTENING

**A.** **LISTEN AND TAKE NOTES** Listen to Part 1 of the panel presentation about the work of the Japanese architect Kengo Kuma. Take notes. Remember to write only important words.

**B.** **LISTEN AND TAKE NOTES** Listen to Part 2 of the presentation about the work of the Austrian architect Friedensreich Hundertwasser. Take notes.

**C.** Complete the summaries with the words and phrases from the boxes. Use your notes to help you. Then listen and check your answers.

**Part 1:**

| | | |
|---|---|---|
| architects | blend in | country |
| materials and colors | to look natural | |

The presentation is about the work of two different ___architects___ (1), Kengo Kuma and Friedensreich Hundertwasser. Both architects want their buildings ________ (2). Kuma often builds in the ________ (3). He makes his buildings ________ (4) with the environment. He does this with the ________ (5) he chooses.

**Part 2:**

| | | |
|---|---|---|
| apartment | bright colors | city |
| different | straight lines | |

Hundertwasser builds most of his buildings in the ________ (6), and he uses a lot of ________ (7), not gray or black. He uses natural shapes and almost no ________ (8). He wants every home to be ________ (9), even if it is part of an ________ (10) building.

**D. Work with a partner. Complete the chart with information about the two architects' buildings. Then listen again and check your answers.**

| | Great Bamboo Wall House | Hundertwasser House |
|---|---|---|
| location | | |
| typical colors | | |
| special features | | |

**E. Read the sentences. Circle the answer that best completes each statement.**

1. The presenter discusses Kuma's work in ____.
   a. Japan and China
   b. Japan and New York
   c. China and New York

2. Kuma's buildings in Tokyo were made of ____.
   a. wood
   b. paper
   c. concrete

3. His Tokyo buildings were usually ____.
   a. green
   b. gray
   c. brown

4. Hundertwasser planted trees ____.
   a. only on the roofs of his buildings
   b. only inside his buildings
   c. on the roofs and inside the buildings

5. Hundertwasser said that the "usual" apartment buildings (not his) made him think of ____.
   a. prisons
   b. nature
   c. factories

6. He called the people who lived in those buildings ____.
   a. green people
   b. gray people
   c. blue people

**F. Read the statements. Write *T* (true) or *F* (false). Then correct the false statements.**

____ 1. For Kuma, the location of a building was not important for the design.

______________________________________________

____ 2. The Great Bamboo Wall House blends in with the mountains around it.

______________________________________________

____ 3. Hundertwasser believed that buildings in the city should be connected to nature.

______________________________________________

____ 4. Hundertwasser didn't allow people in his building to change the colors.

______________________________________________

**G. Work in a group. Look at the two buildings and compare them with the work of Kuma and Hundertwasser. Which reminds you more of Kuma? Which of Hundertwasser? Why?**

**H. Go online to listen to *What Color Is Your Car?* and check your comprehension.**

## SAY WHAT YOU THINK

**A. Discuss the questions in a group.**

1. Which house do you prefer—the Great Bamboo Wall House or Hundertwasser House? Why?
2. What colors are popular for houses where you live? Are there many different colors or are they mostly the same?
3. What does your dream house look like?

**B. Before you watch the video, discuss the questions in a group.**

1. What colors do you prefer for your clothing and for your home?
2. What companies do you identify with a particular color?

**C.** **Go online to watch the video about how corporations use color. Then check your comprehension.**

**VIDEO VOCABULARY**

**consistent** *(adj.)* always behaving in the same way

**corporately** *(adj.)* relating to corporations

**faded** *(adj.)* a color that is lighter or less bright than it originally was

**right on** *(phr.)* correct, accurate

**update** *(v.)* to make something more modern

**D.** **Think about the video, Listening 1, and Listening 2 as you discuss the questions.**

1. How can you compare the way animals use color with the way architects use color?
2. Think about companies and businesses in your community. What colors do you associate with each one? Are there any colors you think would NOT be good for a company? Why?

## Vocabulary Skill | Word families: nouns and verbs

Some words can be used as a **noun** or a **verb**. To know if a word is a noun or a verb, you have to look at the words around it.

There are pictures of the architect's **work** on the Internet. (noun)
The men **work** at the building site every day. (verb)

A word is probably a noun if it comes after . . .

- an article (*a, an,* or *the*).
- an adjective.
- a number.
- the words *this, that, these,* or *those.*

A word may be a verb if it comes after . . .

- a pronoun such as *it* or *they.*
- a time word such as *sometimes* or *never.*
- a helping verb such as *do, does, can, will,* or *should.*

**A.** **Look at the bold word in each sentence. Write *N* (noun) or *V* (verb).**

_V_ 1. We can **camouflage** this birdhouse. We can paint it the same color as the tree.

____ 2. An owl is a bird that flies at night. It calls, "Hoo, hoo, hoo." It **sounds** like it's asking, "Who? Who? Who?"

____ 3. The **poison** of that insect is very strong, but it can't kill a person.

____ 4. There are many different **sounds** in the forest at night.

____ 5. That architect **blends** natural materials and concrete.

____ 6. Both of these shirts are blue, but the colors don't **match**. This one is darker.

____ 7. The color green is actually a **blend** of blue and yellow.

____ 8. That liquid is dangerous. It can **poison** people and animals.

**B. Complete each sentence with the correct word from the box. Then write *N* (noun) or *V* (verb).**

| camouflage | ~~change~~ | fight | match | poison | sound |
|---|---|---|---|---|---|

1. When these birds are young, they are brown and white. When they become adults, their colors ___*change*___ to black and orange. _*V*_
2. When catbirds sing, the __________ is like cats meowing. ____
3. Bowerbirds sometimes __________ other birds for building materials. ____
4. They're trying to __________ the buildings by painting them brown and green. ____
5. Is the red in these shoes a good __________ with the red in my jacket? ____
6. Can the skin of the dart frog __________ me if I touch it? ____

**Tip for Success**

The pronoun *it* refers to both male and female animals. You can also use the pronouns *he* and *she* for animals when you know the gender of the animal.

A blue poison dart frog

**C. Go online for more practice with word families.**

# SPEAKING

**At the end of this unit, you will design a house or an apartment building. Make sure to give examples when you describe the building to group members.**

## Grammar *There's* and *it's*

*There's (There is)* is used when something is being mentioned for the first time.

**There's** a <u>bookstore</u> on campus.
**There's** a <u>software program</u> called Camouflage. It hides your files so others can't find them.
**There's** a <u>tree</u> on the roof of that building!

The pronoun *it* in the expression *it's* (*it is*) refers to something we already know.

The <u>dart frog</u> is bright blue. Predators know that **it's** dangerous.
He lives in a new <u>apartment building</u>. **It's** like a big gray box.

**A. Complete the paragraph with *there's* and *it's*.**

There are many different animals in the park. ___There's___ (1) a bright red bird in a tree. ________ (2) a male cardinal. Nearby ________ (3) a similar bird, but ________ (4) brown, not red. ________ (5) a female cardinal. On a flower, ________ (6) a beautiful orange and black butterfly. ________ (7) a monarch butterfly. Predators can see it easily. But they also know that ________ (8) a dangerous insect. Its wings have a terrible taste. Its color is a warning to predators.

**B. Work with a partner. Imagine that you are in a place in your city. Describe what you see, using *there's* and *it's*. Take turns.**

*A: There's a restaurant on the corner. I think it's an Italian restaurant.*
*B: There's a new exhibition at the museum. It's about the first trip to the moon.*

**C. Go online for more practice with *there's* and *it's*.**

**D. Go online for the grammar expansion.**

## Pronunciation | Schwa /ə/ in unstressed syllables

The **schwa** sound is the most common vowel sound in English. It is the same sound speakers make when they pause and say *Uh*. It is a very relaxed sound. Unstressed syllables often use the schwa. In dictionaries the pronunciation of the schwa is usually shown with the symbol /ə/.

The word *banana* is a good example of the schwa. The first and last syllables have the schwa. Note that the stressed syllable /*næ*/ is longer than the other syllables.

/bə 'næ nə/

The underlined syllables in these words also use the schwa. These are all unstressed syllables. Remember that any vowel can have the schwa sound.

a-<u>ni</u>-<u>mal</u>  poi-<u>son</u>  <u>sur</u>-vive  pre-<u>da</u>-<u>tor</u>  for-<u>est</u>

The schwa is common in unstressed syllables, but it is sometimes used in stressed syllables.

<u>hun</u>-gry  <u>mo</u>-ney

**A. Listen and write the words. There is one unstressed syllable with the schwa sound in each word. Circle the syllable that contains the schwa sound.**

1. camouflage
2. ______
3. ______
4. ______
5. ______
6. ______
7. ______
8. ______

**B. Listen again. Then practice with a partner. Take turns saying the words.**

**C. Listen to these pairs of words. Which word has the schwa sound in the underlined syllable? Circle your answers.**

1. <u>con</u>tain  <u>con</u>crete
2. <u>men</u>tion  apart<u>ment</u>
3. <u>an</u>swer  <u>a</u>nother
4. <u>pro</u>gram  <u>pro</u>tection
5. <u>ma</u>terial  <u>ma</u>ny

**D. Work with a partner. Underline all the syllables with the schwa sound. Then take turns reading the sentences.**

1. Concrete contains a mix of sand, cement, and water.
2. Is there an apartment for rent on State Street?
3. We need to find another answer to the problem.
4. There's a special program to protect the city's water.

**E. Go online for more practice with schwa in unstressed syllables.**

## Speaking Skill | Asking for and giving examples

When you explain something, give **examples** to help the listener understand your ideas. When you don't understand something a speaker says, ask for an example.

**Giving an example:**

For example, . . .
For instance, . . .
Here's an example.

**Asking for an example:**

Can you give me an example?
Do you have any examples?

**A. Listen to the excerpts from the Listenings in this unit. How do the speakers introduce or ask for examples? Write the expressions they use.**

1. ______________________________

______________________________

2. ______________________________

______________________________

3. ______________________________

______________________________

4. ______________________________

______________________________

**B.** **Work with a partner. Choose one of the topics below. Tell your partner about the topic. Take turns asking for and giving examples.**

- the best colors for the rooms of a house
- why I love the colors of the desert (or the mountains, the beach, etc.)
- my favorite colors to wear

**C.** **Go online for more practice with asking for and giving examples.**

## Unit Assignment Present a building design

**In this section, you are going to present a design of a house or an apartment building. As you prepare your design, think about the Unit Question, "How can colors be useful?" Use information from Listening 1, Listening 2, the unit video, and your work in this unit to support your presentation. Refer to the Self-Assessment checklist on page 44.**

1

2

3

4

## CONSIDER THE IDEAS

**Look at the photos on page 42. Then discuss the questions in a group.**

1. Which building do you like the most? Why?
2. Which building do you like the least? Why?
3. Do you like buildings that blend into their environments or buildings that are unusual? Explain.

## PREPARE AND SPEAK

**A. GATHER IDEAS Work in a group. You are going to design a building. Complete the steps.**

1. Decide the type of building. Is it an apartment building or a house?
2. Choose a location for the building. Is your building in a city, a town, or the country? ________________ Our building is in a ___.
   a. desert area: dry without many green plants
   b. forest area: green with a lot of trees
   c. large city: downtown with a lot of people and buildings
   d. large city: quiet street near the edge of the city
   e. beach town: near the ocean

**B. ORGANIZE IDEAS Discuss with your group what the building looks like from the outside. Then create an outline, using the categories below. Use visual elements in your notes to help show what your building looks like.**

- building type
- location
- materials (concrete, wood, glass, metal, etc.)
- outside colors
- plan (how big, how many floors, how many rooms, etc.)
- blends in or is unusual?

**C. SPEAK Present your building design to another group. Refer to the Self-Assessment checklist below before you begin.**

1. Use your outline and visual elements from Activity B to help you.
2. Make sure that each person in the group takes part in the presentation.
3. Give examples and show some visual elements to help your audience to better understand.

**Go online for your alternate Unit Assignment.**

## CHECK AND REFLECT

**A. CHECK Think about the Unit Assignment as you complete the Self-Assessment checklist.**

| SELF-ASSESSMENT | | |
|---|---|---|
| Yes | No | |
| ☐ | ☐ | I used visual elements to show my ideas. |
| ☐ | ☐ | I was able to speak easily about the topic. |
| ☐ | ☐ | My audience understood me. |
| ☐ | ☐ | I used *there's* and *it's*. |
| ☐ | ☐ | I used vocabulary from the unit. |
| ☐ | ☐ | I asked for and gave examples. |
| ☐ | ☐ | I used the schwa in unstressed syllables. |

**B. REFLECT Go to the Online Discussion Board to discuss these questions.**

1. What is something new you learned in this unit?
2. Look back at the Unit Question—How can colors be useful? Is your answer different now than when you started this unit? If yes, how is it different? Why?

# TRACK YOUR SUCCESS

**Circle the words you have learned in this unit.**

**Nouns**
concrete
insect
poison
predator
shape
site AWL
skin
sound
warning
wing

**Verbs**
advise
camouflage
change
fight
hide
match
survive AWL

**Adjectives**
straight
urban

**Phrasal Verbs**
blend in
stand out

Oxford 3000™ words
AWL Academic Word List

**Check (✓) the skills you learned. If you need more work on a skill, refer to the page(s) in parentheses.**

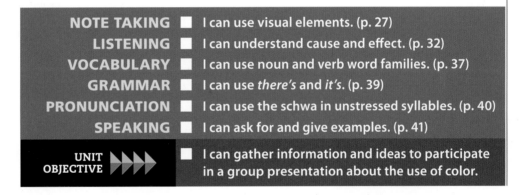

| | | |
|---|---|---|
| **NOTE TAKING** | ■ | I can use visual elements. (p. 27) |
| **LISTENING** | ■ | I can understand cause and effect. (p. 32) |
| **VOCABULARY** | ■ | I can use noun and verb word families. (p. 37) |
| **GRAMMAR** | ■ | I can use *there's* and *it's*. (p. 39) |
| **PRONUNCIATION** | ■ | I can use the schwa in unstressed syllables. (p. 40) |
| **SPEAKING** | ■ | I can ask for and give examples. (p. 41) |
|  **UNIT OBJECTIVE** | ■ | I can gather information and ideas to participate in a group presentation about the use of color. |

Behavioral Science

| | |
|---|---|
| LISTENING | predicting |
| NOTE TAKING | organizing notes |
| VOCABULARY | synonyms |
| GRAMMAR | modal verbs *should* and *shouldn't* |
| PRONUNCIATION | final /s/ or /z/ sounds |
| SPEAKING | giving advice and making recommendations |

UNIT QUESTION

# Why are good manners important?

**A Discuss these questions with your classmates.**

1. Do you feel that people are usually polite? Give examples.
2. Are you ever unsure about manners in social situations? Give examples.
3. Look at the photo. What is the man doing? What do you think of his behavior?

UNIT OBJECTIVE ▶▶▶▶ **Listen to a radio program and a news report. Gather information and ideas to give a presentation about manners.**

**B** **Listen to *The Q Classroom* online. Then answer these questions.**

1. What example does Felix give to show that good manners make people feel good?
2. According to Sophy, how can good manners unite people?

iQ ONLINE **C** **Go online to watch the video about a class on the social skill of making "small talk" at the Massachusetts Institute of Technology (MIT). Then check your comprehension.**

**VIDEO VOCABULARY**

**contentious debate** *(n.)* an angry argument

**failing health** *(n.)* serious illness

**initiate** *(v.)* to start, to begin

**rapport** *(n.)* a good connection with someone

**snippet** *(n.)* a small piece of something

iQ ONLINE **D** **Go to the Online Discussion Board to discuss the Unit Question with your classmates.**

**E** **Complete the survey. Then compare your answers with a partner.**

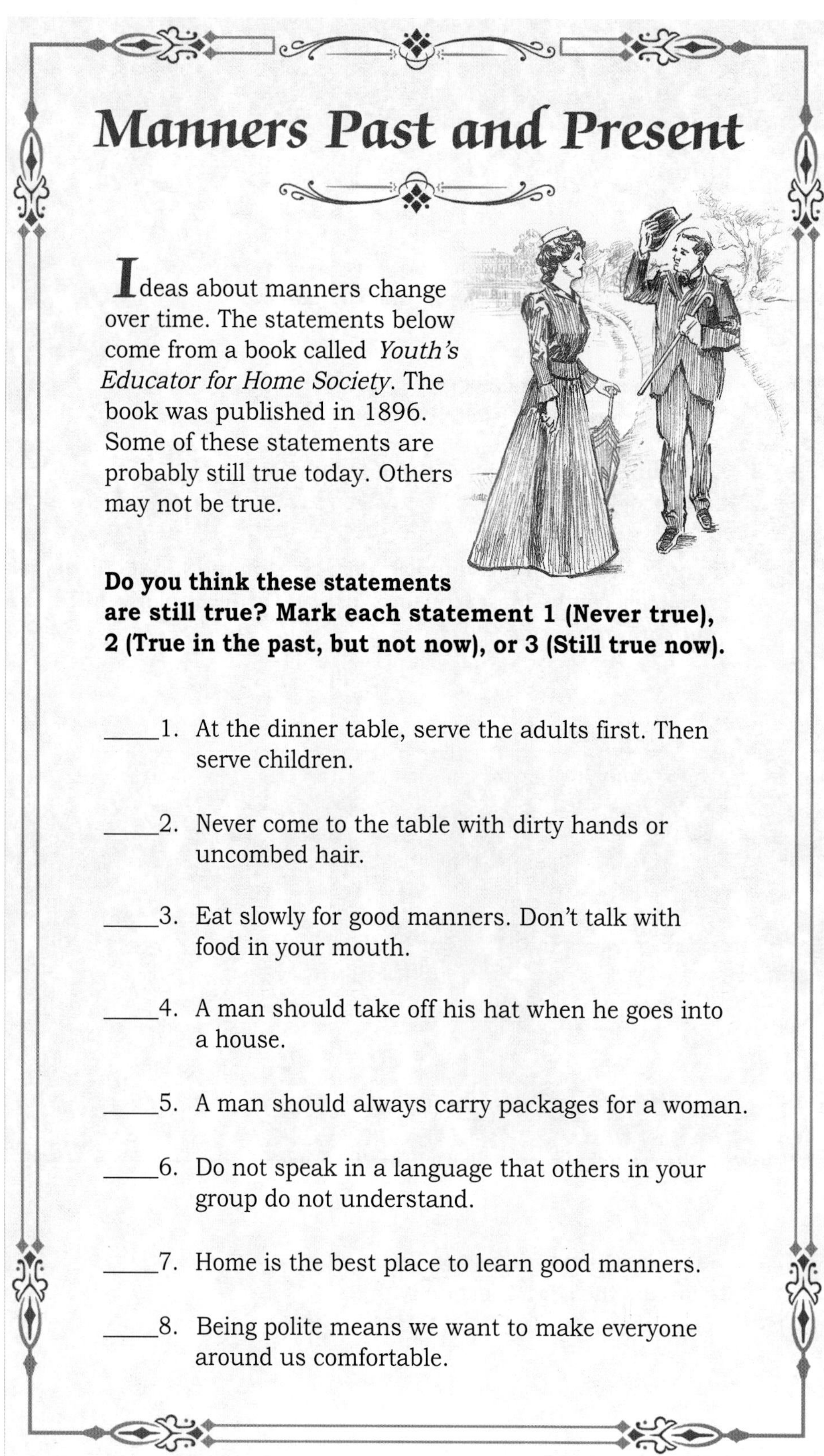

# Manners Past and Present

Ideas about manners change over time. The statements below come from a book called *Youth's Educator for Home Society*. The book was published in 1896. Some of these statements are probably still true today. Others may not be true.

**Do you think these statements are still true? Mark each statement 1 (Never true), 2 (True in the past, but not now), or 3 (Still true now).**

_____1. At the dinner table, serve the adults first. Then serve children.

_____2. Never come to the table with dirty hands or uncombed hair.

_____3. Eat slowly for good manners. Don't talk with food in your mouth.

_____4. A man should take off his hat when he goes into a house.

_____5. A man should always carry packages for a woman.

_____6. Do not speak in a language that others in your group do not understand.

_____7. Home is the best place to learn good manners.

_____8. Being polite means we want to make everyone around us comfortable.

# LISTENING

## LISTENING 1 | Be Polite

**You are going to listen to a radio program called *Book Talk*. The people on the program talk about the book *The Civility Solution: What to Do When People Are Rude* by P. M. Forni. It is about the need for more polite behavior in our society. As you listen to the program, gather information and ideas about why good manners are important.**

### PREVIEW THE LISTENING

**A. VOCABULARY Here are some words from Listening 1. Read the definitions. Then circle the best word to complete each sentence.**

**behavior** (*noun*) 🔑 the way you act
**courtesy** (*noun*) pleasant behavior that shows respect for other people
**etiquette** (*noun*) the rules for courtesy and polite behavior
**manners** (*noun*) 🔑 acceptable behavior in a culture
**polite** (*adjective*) 🔑 having good manners and showing courtesy
**rude** (*adjective*) 🔑 not polite

🔑 Oxford 3000™ words

1. You should always treat co-workers with (behavior / courtesy) and respect. Good manners are important at work.
2. Miteb's (behavior / courtesy) in today's class was terrible. He arrived late, he talked on his cell phone, and then he went to sleep!
3. I'm nervous about dining in the restaurant tonight. There are so many different glasses and forks on the table. Can I borrow your book about (etiquette / behavior)?
4. When you stay at a friend's house, it is (polite / rude) to write them a thank-you note. It shows you are a good friend.
5. That child was very rude to everyone. Parents should teach their kids better (manners / courtesy).

**Vocabulary Skill Review**

In Unit 2, you learned that some words can be used as a noun or a verb. Can any of the underlined words in Activity B be used as both a noun and as a verb? Circle them.

**B. Read the sentences. Then circle the answer that best matches the meaning of each underlined word.**

1. I admit that I made a mistake. I was rude to Sara.
   a. agree it is true
   b. wish it is wrong
2. In that society, it's normal for people to arrive late. Being late is OK in that culture.
   a. a group of people at a school
   b. the people of one country or area
3. One reason for the increase in car accidents is that people don't pay attention to the road.
   a. smaller number
   b. growing number
4. There's too much violence in video games. It's not good to see characters fight and kill.
   a. rude or impolite words
   b. actions done to hurt someone
5. When a soccer player scores a goal, the people in the stadium often scream with excitement. The noise is incredible!
   a. speak in very loud voices
   b. speak very quietly

**C. Go online for more practice with the vocabulary.**

## Listening Skill Predicting

As a listener, you can't always **predict**, or guess, what you are going to hear. There's no way to know what people are going to talk about at an event or what you are going to hear on the street. At other times, you can predict the topic—for example, in a class, on TV, or on the radio. In these cases, you can prepare to listen.

- Find out about the topic. For a radio or TV program, look at the program guide. For a class, check the class schedule or your notes from the last class.
- Ask, "What do I know about this topic?"

For example, if you are going to watch a TV documentary about tigers, you might ask questions like these.

What do I know about tigers?
What do they look like?
Where do they live?

Road rage

**D.** **PREVIEW** **You are going to listen to people on a radio program talk about the need for more polite behavior in our society. What do you think is the best way to respond to a rude person? Discuss your idea with a partner.**

**E.** **Listen to three parts of the radio program. Before you listen to each part, discuss the question with a partner. Predict what the speaker will say. Listen to check your prediction.**

**Part 1** The host of the program is going to introduce his guest. What information do you think he will include?

**Part 2** What question did the host ask at the end of Part 1? How do you think Lynn Hancock will answer this question?

**Part 3** How does the host feel about being polite when others are rude? What will Hancock say about this?

**F.** **Go online for more practice with predicting.**

## WORK WITH THE LISTENING

**A.** **LISTEN AND TAKE NOTES** **Listen to the program again. As you listen, think about these key words. Why is each one important? Use the words in your notes.**

| | |
|---|---|
| bad manners | the "civility solution" |
| increase | journalist |
| polite | road rage |
| rudeness | violence |

**B.** **Read the statements. Write *T* (true) or *F* (false). Use your notes to help you.**

**Tip for Success**

As you listen, try to think ahead. Ask, "What's next? What is the speaker going to say?"

____ 1. Professor Forni says people are more polite now than in the past.

____ 2. Professor Forni says rudeness can cause social problems.

____ 3. Professor Forni says there is no connection between rudeness and stress.

____ 4. The best idea is to be polite when people are rude to you.

____ 5. It's OK to say that you don't like someone's behavior.

**C. Read the sentences. Circle the answer that best completes each statement. Then listen and check your answers.**

1. The host of the program is ___.
   a. Scott Webber
   b. John Hopkins
   c. Lynn Hancock
2. Professor Forni teaches ___ at Johns Hopkins University.
   a. psychology
   b. sociology
   c. literature
3. "Road rage" is a term used to describe drivers who ___.
   a. get angry while driving
   b. are not good drivers
   c. drive too fast
4. If someone is yelling at you, you should ___.
   a. scream at them
   b. say nothing and walk away
   c. stay calm and speak politely
5. Lynn tells a story about something that happened to her when she was ___.
   a. driving her car
   b. riding on a bus
   c. riding on the subway

**D. Lynn Hancock tells a story to show how the "civility solution" worked for her. Work with a partner. Take turns asking and answering the questions.**

1. What happened?
2. Was it an accident or did she do it on purpose?
3. What did the man do?
4. How did Lynn respond?
5. Was the "civility solution" successful in this case?

**E. Work in a group. Read the excerpt from Listening 1 and fill in the missing words. Then listen and check your answers.**

Well, that's where the "civility ________ (1)" comes in. When someone is ________ (2) to us, it's natural, or ________ (3), to be rude to them. You're rude to me, so I'm rude to you. It's a ________ (4) of rudeness. But, when we're ________ (5) to someone who is rude, it ________ (6) the circle. In other ________ (7), you're rude to me, but I'm polite to you. If people can learn to do this, our ________ (8) will be better.

**F. Work with a partner. Choose one of these situations. Create a conversation to practice the civility solution. One person will be A and the other will be B.**

**Situation 1: A meeting of co-workers in an office to discuss ways to make the office a better place to work.**

A: Suggest that workers collect money to buy a coffee machine and coffee and tea supplies for the office.

B: Say that A's idea is "ridiculous."

A: Respond to B. Use the civility solution.

**Situation 2: Two people sitting next to each other on a train. There's a sign above the seats that says "As a courtesy to other passengers, please do not use your cell phone on the train."**

A: You are talking loudly to a friend on your cell phone.

B: Ask A politely to stop talking on the cell phone. Point to the sign.

A: Tell B that you will stop "in a minute," but keep on talking.

B: Ask A to stop talking on the cell phone. Be polite, but firm. Use the civility solution.

## SAY WHAT YOU THINK

**Discuss the questions in a group.**

**Critical Thinking Tip**

In Question 3, you have to **predict** what will happen if people follow Professor Forni's ideas. **Predicting** is figuring out what will happen based on what you know.

1. Think of a time when someone was rude to you. What did you do and say?
2. What do you think of Professor Forni's ideas? Are they easy to follow? Do they work? Why or why not?
3. Imagine that many people start to follow Professor Forni's ideas. Can this change society?

## Note-taking Skill | Organizing notes

When you take notes, it is important to organize the notes on the page. First, write the topic at the top of the page. Do this before the class begins if you can. When the class begins, make a quick outline for your notes. For example, an instructor might say something like, "Today we're going to talk about three ways in which rudeness hurts individuals and our society." This tells you that there are three main points to listen for. If this happens, write the numbers 1, 2, 3 on the page. Leave space after each number to write notes.

Read the introduction to a presentation about the use of color in architecture. Notice that the student wrote a few key words about the topic at the top of the page. The student then prepared space for the two main topics in the discussion and copied the names the instructor wrote on the board.

*Today we're going to discuss the work of two architects and their use of color. First, you will see some examples of the work of the Mexican architect Luis Barragan. Then we'll move on to the work of young French architect Emmanuelle Moureaux. Moureaux's use of happy colors in her work makes some refer to her as a "Joymaker."*

*architecture, use of color*

1. *Luis Barragan* ______________________

   ______________________

   ______________________

2. *Emmanuelle Moureaux* ______________________

   ______________________

   ______________________

**A.** **Listen to the introduction to a talk titled "A History of Rude Behavior." Then prepare a page you could use to take notes.**

**B.** **Compare your note page with a partner. Answer the questions.**

1. How many topics did the speaker mention?
2. How did you describe each topic?

**C.** **Go online for more practice with organizing notes.**

# LISTENING 2 | Classroom Etiquette

**You are going to listen to a news report about teaching etiquette in the classroom. Teachers think that students need to learn better manners. The question is, "Who should teach manners, parents or teachers?" As you listen to the news report, gather information and ideas about why good manners are important.**

## PREVIEW THE LISTENING

**A. VOCABULARY Here are some words and phrases from Listening 2. Read the definitions. Then complete each sentence with the correct word or phrase.**

**attentive** (*adjective*) watching or listening carefully
**courteous** (*adjective*) polite, having courtesy
**deal with** (*phrasal verb*) to solve a problem
**improve** (*verb*) to make something better
**influence** (*noun*) the power to change how someone or something acts
**principal** (*noun*) the person in charge of a school
**respect** (*noun*) consideration for the rights and feelings of other people
**shout out** (*phrasal verb*) to say something in a loud voice
**valuable** (*adjective*) very useful or important

Oxford 3000™ words

1. I apologized to show Sue I have ________________ for her feelings.
2. The parents are meeting with the ________________ tonight to discuss problems at school. She can make new school rules to stop the problems.
3. Parents can have a great ________________ on a child's behavior. They can teach by setting an example.
4. Teachers have to ________________ many difficult problems in the classroom every day. They think of many good solutions.
5. Everyone thought that the class was very ________________. It helped them get better grades and it improved their social skills.
6. I don't like it when people in a meeting just ________________ their comments. They should wait their turn and speak politely.
7. Lisa and Mark want to ________________ their Spanish. They go to class every day and practice often.

8. Young children can only be ________________ for 20 or 30 minutes at a time. It is hard for them to sit still and focus for a long time.

9. Your son is very ________________ at school. He calls me Ms. Moore, and he always says *please* and *thank you*.

iQ ONLINE

**B. Go online for more practice with the vocabulary.**

**C. PREVIEW You are going to listen to a news report about teaching etiquette in the classroom. What do you think parents and teachers say about the etiquette classes? Circle *a* or *b*. Then explain your choice to a partner.**

a. They like the classes. They feel they have a positive effect on the children's behavior.

b. The classes are a waste of time. Kids have to learn good manners at home.

## WORK WITH THE LISTENING

**A. LISTEN AND TAKE NOTES Listen to the first part of the news report about teaching etiquette in the classroom. Prepare a page for note taking. Write a few key words and a short outline.**

**B. Listen to the rest of the news report and take notes. Use the page you prepared in Activity A.**

**C. Read the sentences. Circle the answer that best completes each statement. Use your notes to help you.**

1. The main point of the news report is that ____.
   a. parents don't know how to teach their children good manners
   b. teachers don't have time to teach manners in the classroom
   c. some schools teach manners in the classroom

2. According to Marjorie Lucas, the most important idea about manners is that ____.
   a. children need to respect other people
   b. fighting and violence are bad
   c. children need to have good table manners

3. The report makes it clear that ____.
   a. parents are better than schools at teaching manners
   b. the results of the etiquette classes surprised teachers
   c. the etiquette classes helped children, teachers, and parents

**D. Work with a partner. Try to find information in your notes about each of these items. Listen again and add to your notes, if necessary.**

1. one example of polite behavior for children around adults

   Use titles like Mr., Mrs., and Ms.

2. the name of the company that teaches etiquette classes

   ______________________________

3. one example of good behavior at school

   ______________________________

4. two positive results from the etiquette classes

   ______________________________

   ______________________________

5. how parents feel about the etiquette classes

   ______________________________

**E. Listen to these sentences from the news report. Circle the sentence closest in meaning to the one you hear.**

1. a. When teachers have to spend time dealing with bad behavior, they have less time to teach other things.
   b. For teachers, dealing with bad behavior is the most important part of their job.
2. a. When children do small things, like saying "please" and "thank you," it shows that they have respect for others.
   b. Children can be courteous in small ways, but that doesn't mean they respect other people.
3. a. Students earned good grades in the etiquette classes during the school year.
   b. Because of the etiquette classes, students got better grades in their class work.
4. a. Students listen more carefully when they are in class.
   b. Students aren't absent from class as much as they were in the past.

**F.** **Look at the list of rules that a teacher made for the classroom. Complete each sentence on the list with a phrase from the box. Then add one more "rule" to the list. Use your own idea.**

| | |
|---|---|
| get into fights | Mr., Ms., or Mrs. |
| raise your hand | say "Excuse me" |
| say "Please" | say "Thank you" |
| shout out the answer | |

### Classroom Rules

1. When you want to answer a question, ___raise your hand___.
2. Don't ________________ when I ask a question.
3. When you speak to teachers or to the principal, use ________________ and their last name.
4. If you bump into someone, ________________.
5. When you ask for something, ________________.
6. Don't ________________ in the hallway or on the playground.
7. When someone gives you something, ________________.
8. ________________________________

**G.** **Go online to listen to *Phone Interview Etiquette* and check your comprehension.**

## SAY WHAT YOU THINK

**A.** **Discuss the questions in a group.**

1. Is it true that parents today are not teaching good manners to their children? Why or why not?
2. How did you learn about manners or etiquette? Give examples.

**B. Think about the video, Listening 1, and Listening 2 as you discuss the questions.**

1. What would Professor Forni think about companies giving etiquette classes in schools?
2. Do you agree that the ability to make small talk is an important social skill? Why or why not? Give examples to support your opinion.

## Vocabulary Skill Synonyms

Words with the same or very similar meanings are called **synonyms**. Synonyms can make your speaking and writing more interesting.

Dictionaries show the meanings of synonyms, and they provide helpful examples about how to use synonyms.

Dictionaries often give synonyms at the end of entries, and the example sentences at different entries show you how to use the words correctly. For example, look at these definitions of the words *anger* and *rage*. *Anger* and *rage* are synonyms, but *rage* is a stronger feeling than *anger*.

**an·ger**[1] /ˈæŋɡər/ *noun* [U] the strong feeling that you have when something has happened or someone has done something that you do not like: *He could not hide his anger at the news.* ◆ *She was shaking with anger.*

**rage**[1] /reɪdʒ/ *noun* [C, U] a feeling of violent anger that is difficult to control: *He was trembling with rage.* ◆ *to fly into a rage*



**A. Match each word on the left with a synonym on the right. Use your dictionary to help you.**

| | |
|---|---|
| ____ 1. courteous | a. growth |
| ____ 2. rude | b. often |
| ____ 3. scream | c. impolite |
| ____ 4. valuable | d. polite |
| ____ 5. etiquette | e. actions |
| ____ 6. increase | f. yell |
| ____ 7. frequently | g. manners |
| ____ 8. behavior | h. important |

**B.** **Synonyms work well in these sentences. Rewrite each sentence using a synonym for the word or words in bold.**

1. I think it's **rude** to use your cell phone on the bus.

   I think it's impolite to use your cell phone on the bus.

2. Please tell the kids outside to stop **screaming**. My students are taking a test.

   ________________________________________

3. If salespeople are **courteous**, they'll probably make more sales.

   ________________________________________

4. Don't listen to what he says. His **actions** can tell you more than his words.

   ________________________________________

5. Emily Post wrote many books about **good manners**.

   ________________________________________

**C.** **Go online for more practice with synonyms.**

# SPEAKING

**At the end of this unit, you are going to work in a group to give a presentation about using manners in a particular situation. As part of the presentation, you will have to give advice about what people should and should not do in the situation.**

## Grammar Modal verbs *should* and *shouldn't*

Use **should** and **shouldn't** to give and ask for *advice* and *recommendations.*

**Affirmative:** You **should** be polite, even when someone is rude to you.
You **should** wear a suit and tie to the interview.

**Negative:** We **shouldn't** let people say rude things to us.
You **shouldn't** speak Spanish when Ron is here. He doesn't understand it.

**Questions:** **Should** our listeners read the book?
What **should** we do about the kids who wrote on the wall at school?

**A. Complete each sentence with *should* or *shouldn't*. Use your own opinions.**

1. Your best friend thinks she is sending an email to her parents. She sends it to you by mistake. You ________________ read it.
2. A woman ________________ open the door for a man carrying a large box.
3. Children ________________ call their teachers by their first names.
4. University students ________________ raise their hands to ask a question in class.
5. You ________________ call people after 10:00 p.m.
6. Men ________________ stand up when a woman comes into the room.
7. You ________________ tell someone if they have spinach in their teeth.
8. You're sitting on a crowded bus. An older woman gets on. You ________________ offer her your seat.

**B.** **Work with a partner. Take turns asking and answering *Yes/No* questions based on the sentences in Activity A. Explain your answers.**

*A: Should you read your friend's email to her parents?*

*B: No, you shouldn't. You should tell your friend about it.*

**C.** **Go online for more practice with modal verbs *should* and *shouldn't*.**

**D.** **Go online for the grammar expansion.**

## Pronunciation | Final /s/ or /z/ sounds

Words ending in /s/ or /z/ sounds link, or connect, to words beginning with a vowel. Listen to these examples.

It's easy to learn to play chess.

The man was mad at the other drivers around him.

**A.** **Read the sentences. Mark the /s/ and /z/ sounds that link to vowels.**

**Tip for Success**

Learning how to link words will make your speech sound more natural and fluent. It can also make it easier to pronounce final sounds clearly.

1. The students admitted they made a mistake.
2. Parents are too busy to teach their children manners.
3. The book talks about different ways to deal with problems.
4. Bad manners are a problem in our office.
5. I was amazed by my visit to the Great Wall.
6. Is it possible for them to deal with the problem today?

**B.** **Work with a partner. Practice saying the sentences in Activity A. Listen and check your pronunciation.**

**C.** **Listen to the paragraph about the etiquette of hats. Complete the paragraph with the words you hear. Then read the story to a partner.**

Franklin D. Roosevelt, 1944

John F. Kennedy, 1963

## The Etiquette of Hats

There are a lot of ______ (1) about ______ (2) in etiquette books. ______ (3) ______ (4), men and women always wore ______ (5) ______ (6). It was bad ______ (7) to go out without a hat. Men took off their ______ (8) ______ (9). It ______ (10) ______ (11) sign of respect for a man to take off his hat. These rules started to change in the 1960s. John F. Kennedy was the first U.S. president to appear in public without a hat.

**D. Go online for more practice with final /s/ or /z/ sounds.**

## Speaking Skill | Giving advice and making recommendations

When you give **advice** or make **recommendations**, you don't want the listener to think that you're giving commands. To make sure the listener understands, you can use expressions like these.

I think you should . . .
I don't think you should . . .
Don't you think you should . . . ?
Maybe you shouldn't . . .

**A. Work with a partner. Read the sentences. Take turns giving advice.**

1. A: It is hard to get to class on time. What should I do?

   B: I think you should ...

2. A: My homework is very messy. It is difficult for the teacher to read.

   B: Don't you think you should ... ?

3. A: Alan invited me to his house for dinner, but I don't know anybody there!

   B: Maybe you should/shouldn't ...

4. A: My friends send me text messages when I'm in class. It's hard to pay attention in class when they send me messages.

   B: Well, I don't think that you should ...

**B.** **Work with a partner. Choose one of the topics below. Ask your partner for advice. Then give your partner advice about the problem he or she chooses.**

1. You are going to a formal dinner at someone's home. Ask for advice about what to wear, what time to arrive, what to bring, what to talk about with guests, and table manners.

2. You are in charge of a committee. The committee's job is to improve your workplace or classroom. The goal is to encourage people to be more courteous to each other. Ask for advice about what the committee should do.

**C.** **Go online for more practice with giving advice and making recommendations.**

## Unit Assignment Give a presentation on manners

**In this section, you are going to give a short presentation about manners. As you prepare your presentation, think about the Unit Question, "Why are good manners important?" Use information from Listening 1, Listening 2, the unit video, and your work in this unit to support your presentation. Refer to the Self-Assessment checklist on page 66.**

### CONSIDER THE IDEAS

**Read the list of statements and check (✓) the ones you agree with.**

- ☐ People don't always need to have good manners.
- ☐ I think people should learn proper etiquette.
- ☐ Manners should be taught at home, not at school.
- ☐ I prefer to be with people who have good manners.
- ☐ People should know how to behave at all times.
- ☐ Good table manners are not very important.

### PREPARE AND SPEAK

**A.** **GATHER IDEAS** **Work in a group. Choose one presentation topic from the box or think of your own topic.**

| Bad manners for . . . |
| --- |
| • children at home<br>• driving a car<br>• eating with family or friends<br>• riding on a train or bus<br>• students in the classroom |

**B. ORGANIZE IDEAS Prepare a short presentation on the topic your group picked in Activity A. Use the outline to help you organize your ideas. Give at least two examples.**

Topic: Bad manners for ______________________________

1. What some people do: ______________________________

   Why is this an example of bad manners?

   Reasons:

   a. ______________________________

   b. ______________________________

   What people should do: ______________________________

   Reasons:

   a. ______________________________

   b. ______________________________

2. What some people do: ______________________________

   Why is this an example of bad manners?

   Reasons:

   a. ______________________________

   b. ______________________________

   What people should do: ______________________________

   Reasons:

   a. ______________________________

   b. ______________________________

**C.** **SPEAK** **Present your ideas to the class or to another group. Refer to the Self-Assessment checklist below before you begin.**

1. Make sure each member of your group presents at least one idea in the presentation. For example, one person can describe an example of bad manners.

2. In your presentation, explain:
   - why you chose the topic.
   - examples of bad manners.
   - why the behaviors are bad.
   - how people should behave.

**Go online for your alternate Unit Assignment.**

## CHECK AND REFLECT

**A.** **CHECK** **Think about the Unit Assignment as you complete the Self-Assessment checklist.**

| SELF-ASSESSMENT | | |
|---|---|---|
| Yes | No | |
| ☐ | ☐ | I was able to speak easily about the topic. |
| ☐ | ☐ | My partner, group, class understood me. |
| ☐ | ☐ | I used *should* and *shouldn't*. |
| ☐ | ☐ | I used vocabulary from the unit. |
| ☐ | ☐ | I gave advice and I made recommendations. |
| ☐ | ☐ | I connected final /s/ and /z/ sounds to vowels. |

**B.** **REFLECT** **Go to the Online Discussion Board to discuss these questions.**

1. What is something new you learned in this unit?

2. Look back at the Unit Question—Why are good manners important? Is your answer different now than when you started this unit? If yes, how is it different? Why?

# TRACK YOUR SUCCESS

**Circle the words you have learned in this unit.**

| **Nouns** | **Verbs** | **Adverbs** |
|---|---|---|
| actions 🔑 | admit 🔑 | frequently 🔑 |
| anger 🔑 | improve 🔑 | often 🔑 |
| behavior 🔑 | scream 🔑 | **Phrasal Verbs** |
| courtesy | yell | deal with |
| etiquette | **Adjectives** | shout out |
| growth 🔑 | attentive | **Modal Verbs** |
| increase 🔑 | courteous | should 🔑 |
| influence 🔑 | impolite | shouldn't |
| manners 🔑 | important 🔑 | |
| principal 🔑 AWL | polite 🔑 | |
| rage | rude 🔑 | |
| respect 🔑 | valuable 🔑 | |
| society 🔑 | | |
| violence 🔑 | | |

🔑 Oxford 3000™ words

AWL Academic Word List

**Check (✓) the skills you learned. If you need more work on a skill, refer to the page(s) in parentheses.**

| | | |
|---|---|---|
| **LISTENING** | ■ | I can predict. (p. 50) |
| **NOTE TAKING** | ■ | I can organize notes. (p. 54) |
| **VOCABULARY** | ■ | I can use synonyms. (p. 59) |
| **GRAMMAR** | ■ | I can use the modal verbs *should* and *shouldn't*. (p. 61) |
| **PRONUNCIATION** | ■ | I can connect final /s/ or /z/ sounds. (p. 62) |
| **SPEAKING** | ■ | I can give advice and make recommendations. (p. 63) |
| **UNIT OBJECTIVE** ▶▶▶▶ | ■ | I can gather information and ideas to give a presentation about manners. |

UNIT 4

Game Studies

| | | |
|---|---|---|
| NOTE TAKING | ▶ | reviewing and editing notes |
| LISTENING | ▶ | listening for names and dates |
| VOCABULARY | ▶ | word families: suffixes |
| GRAMMAR | ▶ | imperative verbs |
| PRONUNCIATION | ▶ | word stress |
| SPEAKING | ▶ | giving instructions |

UNIT QUESTION

# How can games compare to real life?

**A Discuss these questions with your classmates.**

1. "Life is a game." Do you agree with this statement? Why or why not?
2. How much time do you spend playing games?
3. Look at the photo. What are the people doing? What is happening on the field?

**B Listen to *The Q Classroom* online. Then answer these questions.**

1. What connections did Marcus and Felix find between sports like soccer and real life?
2. What does Sophy say about following rules?

**C Go to the Online Discussion Board to discuss the Unit Question with your classmates.**

UNIT OBJECTIVE ▶▶▶▶ Listen to a talk and a conversation. Gather information and ideas to develop and present an educational board game.

**D** **Work in a group. Discuss these questions.**

1. What games did you play as child? What games do you play now?
2. Games are fun. What are some other reasons to play games?

**E** **Play this game with a partner.**

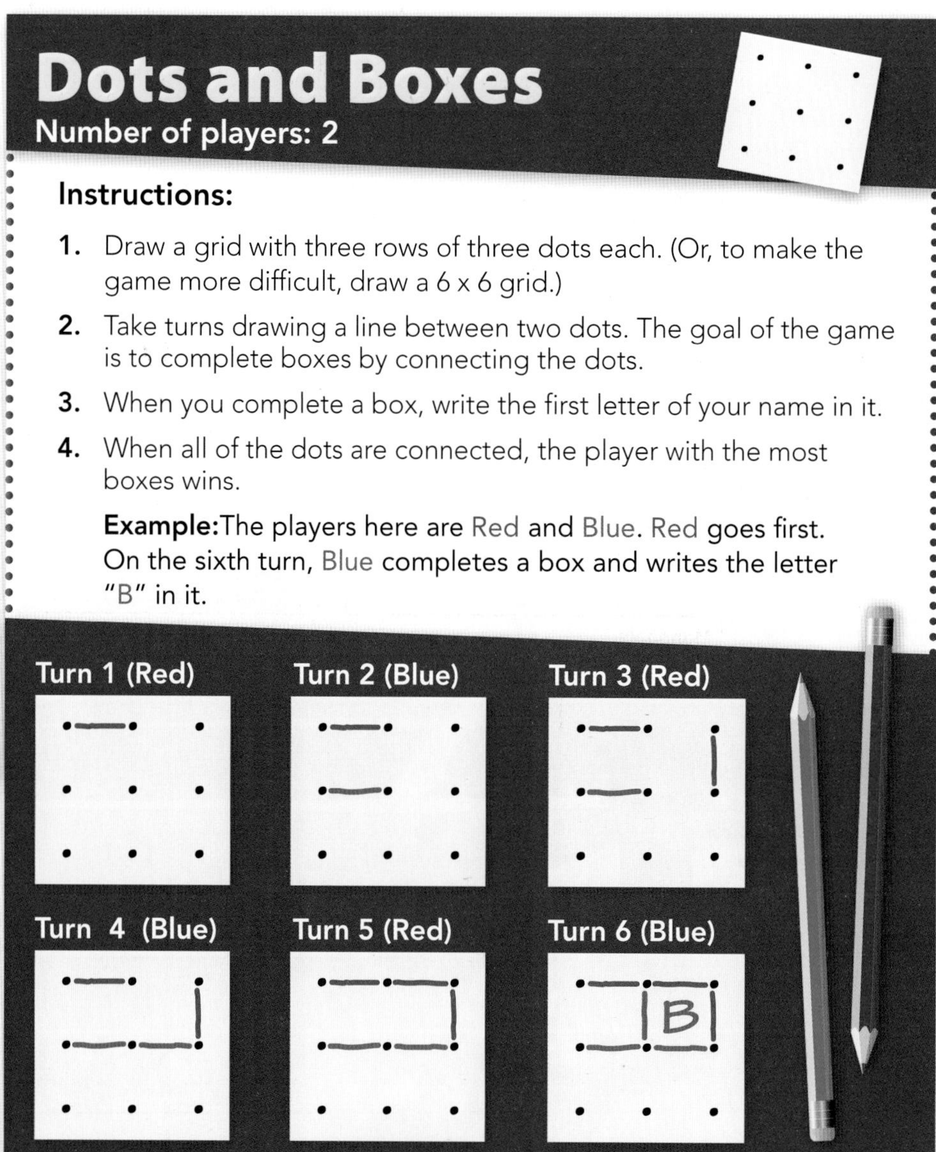

Dots and Boxes
Number of players: 2
Instructions:
1. Draw a grid with three rows of three dots each. (Or, to make the game more difficult, draw a 6 x 6 grid.)
2. Take turns drawing a line between two dots. The goal of the game is to complete boxes by connecting the dots.
3. When you complete a box, write the first letter of your name in it.
4. When all of the dots are connected, the player with the most boxes wins.
Example: The players here are Red and Blue. Red goes first. On the sixth turn, Blue completes a box and writes the letter "B" in it.
Turn 1 (Red)
Turn 2 (Blue)
Turn 3 (Red)
Turn 4 (Blue)
Turn 5 (Red)
Turn 6 (Blue)
B


**F** **What real-life skills did you use to play this game? For example, did you plan ahead? Did you try to guess your partner's moves?**

## Note-taking Skill | Reviewing and editing notes

It is important to review your notes as soon as possible after taking them. When you take notes, you write only single words and short phrases. If you wait too long, you might forget what these mean or why they are important. As you review your notes, edit them and add more information. Your notes will then be a more useful tool for studying. Note: It is a good idea to leave space on the page when you take notes, so you can add more information later.

**A. Listen to a short talk about the board game Monopoly. Then review one student's notes. Fill in the blanks and add other information you remember.**

Monopoly

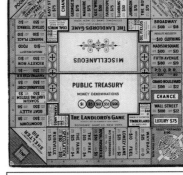

Lizzie Magie's Landlord

***Monopoly***

*A. About game*

*3rd most pop. game*

*about buy and* ____________________

*players pay rent when* ____________________

*Goal = win* ____________________

*B. History*

*Invent Charles Darrow 19* __________

*Darrow get idea earlier game:* ____________________

____________________ *Lizzie Magie 1903*

*Different rules:* ____________________ *pay rent Public Treasury*

*All players get share* ____________________

*C. Conclusion*

____________________

**B. Compare your notes with a partner. Listen again, if necessary.**

**C. Go online for more practice with reviewing and editing notes.**

# LISTENING

## LISTENING 1 | Crossword Puzzles

**You are going to listen to a game developer give a talk about the history of the crossword puzzle. As you listen to the lecture, gather information and ideas about how games can compare to real life.**

### PREVIEW THE LISTENING

**Vocabulary Skill Review**

In Unit 3, you learned about synonyms. Can you find any synonyms for the underlined words in Activity A? Circle them.

**A. VOCABULARY Here are some words from Listening 1. Read the sentences. Then circle the answer that best matches the meaning of each underlined word.**

1. A developer needs special skills to make computer games. He or she has to know a lot about computer programming.
   a. game creator
   b. game seller

2. I don't need an instant answer to my question. You can tell me next week.
   a. correct
   b. immediate

3. The object of this activity is to practice speaking English in a group.
   a. goal or purpose
   b. place or thing

4. The police have several clues to help them solve the crime, for example, a record of phone calls and some fingerprints.
   a. people who work on a criminal investigation
   b. pieces of information or evidence used in an investigation

5. That is the original draft of my essay. I revised it many times. You need to read the final draft instead.
   a. last or newest
   b. first or earliest

6. The new version of this game has more question cards than the old game. It also has different game pieces and a new game board.
   a. cost of a thing
   b. type of a thing



Oxford 3000™ words

7. I need to update my computer. Many of its programs are old and slow. I can buy new ones that work better and faster.
   a. make more current or modern
   b. make bigger or taller

8. I always thought video games were silly, but now I realize they can be a lot fun.
   a. understand for the first time
   b. know nothing about something

**B. Go online for more practice with the vocabulary.**

**C. PREVIEW You are going to listen to a game developer talk about the history of the crossword puzzle. Look at the photos. How is the 1913 "word-cross" puzzle different from later crossword puzzles?**

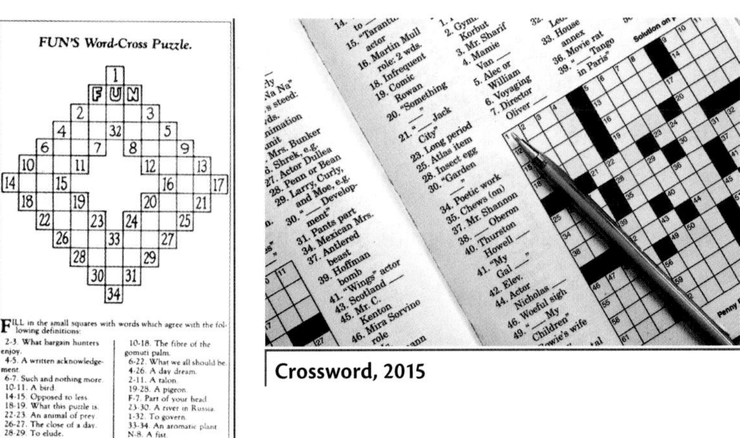


Word-Cross, 1913

Crossword, 2015

## WORK WITH THE LISTENING

**A. LISTEN AND TAKE NOTES Listen to the game developer's talk. Take notes. Use the headings below to help you. Leave space to add more information later.**

**Tip for Success**

When listening to a speech or lecture, sit slightly forward in your seat. This position will help you concentrate, and you will understand more.

Intro / topic
Giuseppe Airoldi
Arthur Wynne
Benefits of crosswords

**B. Work with a partner. Review and compare your notes. Edit them and add more information based on what you remember. Then listen again.**

**C. Read the statements. Write *T* (true) or *F* (false). Then correct the false statements.**

____ 1. The focus of this part of Alex Vargas's speech is his new word game.

____ 2. Crosswords and similar word puzzles have a long history.

____ 3. Crossword puzzles were very popular in the early 1900s.

____ 4. The only reason to do a crossword is that it is fun.

____ 5. Alex Vargas's new game is a modern version of the crossword puzzle.

**D. Read the questions. Circle the correct answers. Then listen and check your answers.**

1. What is Alex Vargas's job?
   a. He writes stories for newspapers.
   b. He writes books about the history of games.
   c. He writes word games for newspapers.

2. When did Giuseppe Airoldi invent his small crossword puzzle?
   a. 1913
   b. 1890
   c. 1819

3. What did Arthur Wynne call his first puzzle?
   a. Word Square
   b. Word-Cross
   c. Cross-Word

4. What was Arthur Wynne's profession?
   a. journalist
   b. librarian
   c. publisher

5. How was Wynne's first puzzle different from his later crossword puzzles?
   a. It had no black squares.
   b. It was in the shape of a square.
   c. It didn't have any clues.

6. What were crossword puzzle fans using at the New York Public Library?
   a. newspapers
   b. magazines
   c. dictionaries

7. Why do people say that crossword puzzles are more than fun and games?
   a. They make our bodies healthier.
   b. They are very difficult to solve.
   c. They make our brains more active.

8. What is the name of Alex Vargas's new game?
   a. Cross Purposes
   b. Social Crossword
   c. Word-Cross

**E. Work in a group. Solve the crossword. All of the words are in this unit.**

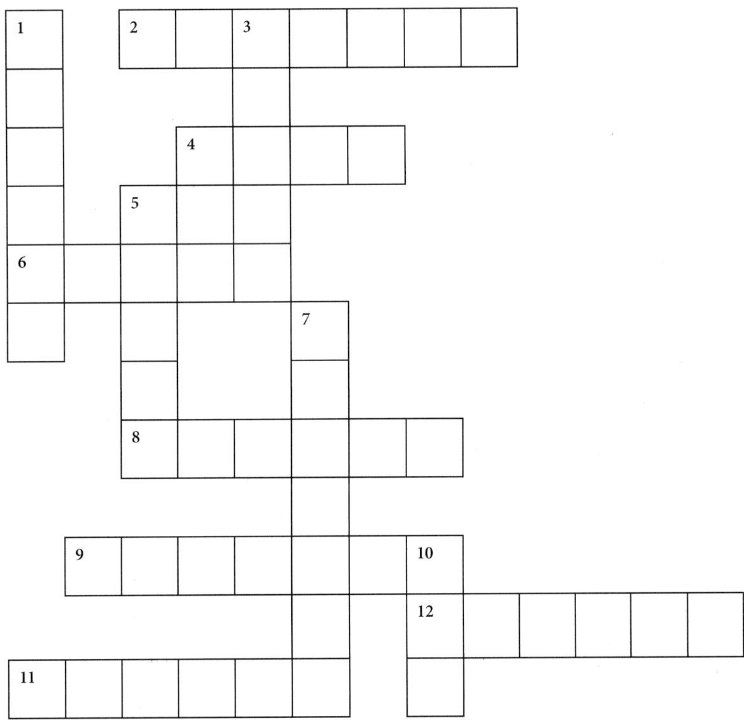

| Across | Down |
|---|---|
| **2.** It was an ____ success. | **1.** The words go ____ and down. |
| **4.** I like playing that video ____. | **3.** What ____ was it? A circle? |
| **6.** Can you ____ the puzzle? | **5.** There are 12 ____ in this puzzle. |
| **8.** Write "A" in the first blank ____. | **7.** to know something for the first time |
| **9.** There's now a new ____ of the game. | **10.** in the present |
| **11.** to make something more modern | |
| **12.** the purpose of a game | |

## SAY WHAT YOU THINK

**Discuss the questions in a group.**

1. Do you enjoy doing crossword puzzles or other word puzzles? Why or why not?
2. What other puzzles and games can you find in newspapers?
3. Crossword puzzles and other puzzles such as Sudoku are now available online. Do you prefer to do puzzles online or in the traditional way with pencil and paper?

## Listening Skill | Listening for names and dates

**Names** and **dates** are often important details when you are listening, whether a friend is telling you a story or you're listening to a news report or a lecture.

- Pay attention to names and dates as you listen and try to remember why they are important.
- If possible, write down names and dates with brief notes to remind you why they are important.

**A. Look at the names and dates in the box. Listen to the information about the word game SCRABBLE™. Then complete each sentence with the correct word.**

Scrabble™

| 1938 | 1948 | 1952 | 1991 | 2006 |
|---|---|---|---|---|
| Alfred Mosher Butts | | James Brunot | | Michael Cresta |

1. Alfred Mosher Butts invented the game of SCRABBLE™ in __________.
2. In __________, Butts and his partner started a SCRABBLE™ factory.
3. Butts's partner was __________.
4. Between __________ and 2000, SCRABBLE™ sold more than 100 million games.
5. The first World SCRABBLE™ Championship was in __________.
6. __________ holds the official record for getting the most points in one game.
7. In __________, he scored 830 points in one game.

**B. Work with a partner. Practice listening for names and dates.**

1. Make a list with three names and three dates that are important to you.
2. Tell your partner about each one. As you speak, your partner should take notes.
3. Ask your partner questions to see if he or she has understood the names and dates.

**C. Go online for more practice with listening for names and dates.**

## LISTENING 2 | Business Is a Game

**You are going to listen to two friends, Waleed and Faisal, talking about an online game. Waleed is playing the game as part of an assignment for a business class. As you listen to the conversation, gather information and ideas about how games can compare to real life.**

### PREVIEW THE LISTENING

**A. VOCABULARY Here are some words from Listening 2. Read the definitions. Then complete the paragraph with the correct words.**

**calculate** (*verb*) 🔑 to find an answer by using mathematics
**demand** (*noun*) 🔑 the need for something among a group of people
**estimate** (*verb*) 🔑 to guess the number, cost, or size of something
**figure out** (*phrasal verb*) to find an answer to something
**loss** (*noun*) 🔑 in business, having less money than when you started
**profit** (*noun*) 🔑 money made by selling something
**sold out** (*phrase*) nothing is left to sell; everything has been sold
**supplies** (*noun*) 🔑 things people need in order to do or make something

🔑 Oxford 3000™ words

#### Community Yard Sales

A business can be like a game. Imagine selling things at a community yard sale, for example. It's a lot of fun, and it's a great way to make extra money on the weekend. Here are a few tips for success. First, you need to ____*figure out*____ (1) what to sell. What old stuff do you have

A community yard sale

that you don't want anymore? What do people want to buy? If there's no ____________ (2) for old coffee pots, for example, don't bring any! The only ____________ (3) you need to have are a box for the money, a table, and a couple of chairs. Then you have to play a little guessing game. You need to ____________ (4) what people can pay for your items and put a price on each one. Don't make the prices too high or too low.

To ____________ (5) if you made money, subtract your costs—what you paid for your supplies—from your sales. Is the result a positive number? If it is, you made a ____________ (6). Is it a negative number? Too bad! You have a ____________ (7) for the day. If you're lucky, you can sell everything. If you're ____________ (8), you don't have to take anything back home with you.

**B.** **Go online for more practice with the vocabulary.**

**C.** **PREVIEW** **You are going to listen to a conversation about an online game. Do you think video games can help you learn skills, such as how to run a business? Why or why not? Discuss with a partner.**

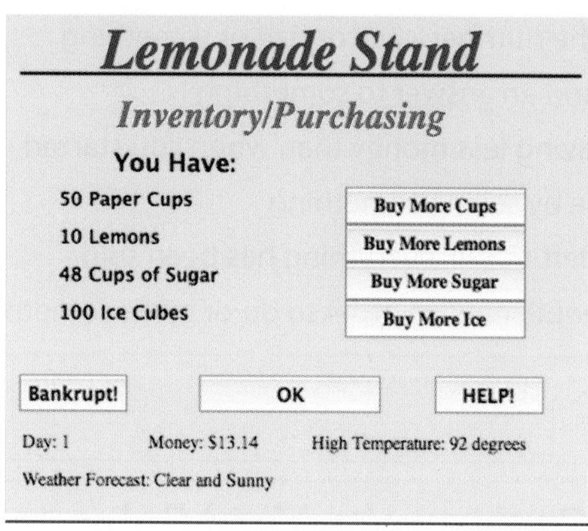


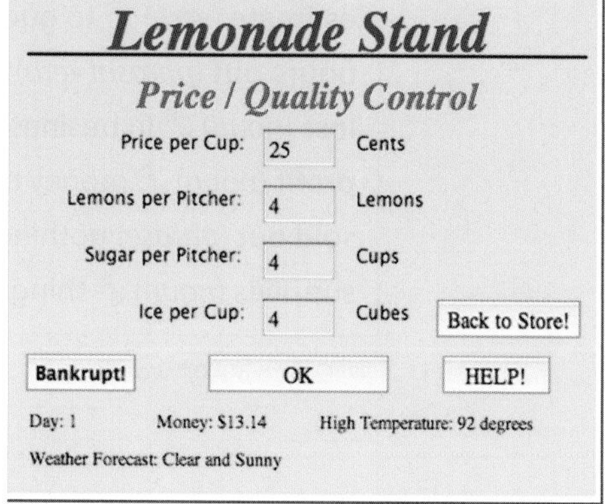


## WORK WITH THE LISTENING

**A.** **LISTEN AND TAKE NOTES** **The two speakers in the conversation, Faisal and Waleed, have different opinions of using the lemonade game for a business class. Listen and write key words to describe each person's opinion. Make two columns for your notes—one for Faisal, and one for Waleed.**

**B. Listen again and take more notes. Use these headings on your paper.**

*How to play the game*

*What students can learn from the game*

*Faisal's and Waleed's conclusions*

**C. Read the questions. Circle the correct answers. Use your notes to help you.**

1. What does Waleed think about the lemonade game?
   a. It's fun, but it can't help him learn about business.
   b. It isn't very interesting, but it can teach him about business.
   c. It's entertaining and useful for learning about business.

2. Which of these things can you learn from the lemonade game?
   a. the connection between supply and demand
   b. how to make good lemonade
   c. a good location for a lemonade stand

3. What happened when Faisal played the game?
   a. He made a profit.
   b. He lost a little money.
   c. He made too much lemonade.

4. What is Faisal's opinion of using a game to learn business?
   a. He thinks it is a good way to learn.
   b. He thinks it only works for lemonade businesses.
   c. He thinks it is not the best idea for a university class.

**D. Read the statements. Write *T* (true) or *F* (false). Then correct the false statements.**

____ 1. In the game, the supplies are paper cups, lemons, sugar, and ice.

______________________________________________

____ 2. There is more demand for lemonade on cloudy days.

______________________________________________

____ 3. Waleed recommends using four lemons and one cup of sugar in each pitcher of lemonade.

______________________________________________

____ 4. The program calculates your profit or loss for each day.

______________________________________________

____ 5. The decisions you make in the game are very different from the decisions in a real business.

______________________________________________

____ 6. At the end, Faisal says the game is great for a university class.

______________________________________________

**E. Work with a partner. Take turns asking and answering the questions.**

1. What happens if a player buys too much ice or too many lemons in one day?
2. Why does the game include a weather forecast at the bottom of the screen?
3. What do players need to think about when deciding on a price for the lemonade?
4. What happens in the game if a player doesn't make enough lemonade?

**F. Work with a partner. Frank played the lemonade game for four days. Complete his spreadsheet with the profit or loss for each day. Then answer the questions.**

| Frank's Lemonade Stand | Thursday (Cloudy / 86) | Friday (Rain / 67) | Saturday (Sunny / 94) | Sunday (Cloudy / 77) |
|---|---|---|---|---|
| **Money at start of day** | $20.00 | $15.72 | $15.80 | $23.66 |
| **Expenses** | | | | |
| Cups /ice | $5.30 | $1.72 | $3.87 | $2.95 |
| Lemons/sugar | $7.38 | 0 | $2.77 | $3.18 |
| **Total expenses** | $12.68 | $1.72 | $6.64 | $6.13 |
| **Price per cup** | $0.30 | $0.20 | $0.25 | $0.25 |
| **Sales** | $8.40 | $1.80 | $14.50 (SOLD OUT!) | $7.00 |
| **Profit or loss** | ($4.28) | | | |

1. On which day did Frank lose the most money? Why do you think that happened?
2. On which day did he make the biggest profit? Why?
3. How much was Frank's total profit for his four days?
4. Did Frank make any mistakes as he played the game? For example, was it a good idea to charge $0.30 a cup on Thursday, his first day?

**G. Go online to listen to *Games for Creativity* and check your comprehension.**

## SAY WHAT YOU THINK

**A. Discuss the questions in a group.**

1. Waleed and Faisal disagree about how much the lemonade game helps business students. Do you agree with Waleed or Faisal? Why?
2. What other games do people use to practice or train for real-life activities like sports or jobs?

**B. Before you watch the video, discuss the questions in a group.**

1. Did your teachers ever use games in the classroom? If so, what kinds of games? What subjects did the games relate to?
2. What games can be helpful for learning a language?

**C. Go online to watch the video about a teacher who uses games to help students learn about money and business. Then check your comprehension.**

**grasp** *(v.)* understand

**investing** *(n.)* buying property or shares in a company to make money

**majority** *(n.)* the largest part of a group of people or things

**returns on their investments** *(n. phr.)* money made from investing

**D. Think about the video, Listening 1, and Listening 2 as you discuss the questions.**

1. Think about a game or sport you play frequently. What lessons does it teach you about life?
2. Imagine that a parent is complaining that Mary Sandiford, the teacher in the video, is wasting time by using games in the classroom. What would you say to the parent?

## Vocabulary Skill | Word families: suffixes

A **suffix** is a word or syllable(s) placed after a root word. A suffix often changes the part of speech of the word. For example, the suffixes *-(t)y* and *-(c)ity* sometimes mark the change from an *adjective* to a *noun*.

| Adjective | Noun |
|---|---|
| honest | honesty |
| popular | popularity |
| simple | simplicity |

Note: the silent *e* in *simple* is dropped before the suffix is added.

**A. Complete the chart with the noun forms of these words. Use the suffixes *-(t)y* or *-(c)ity*. Use a dictionary to help you.**

| Adjective | Noun |
|---|---|
| active | |
| creative | |
| difficult | |
| real | |
| safe | |

**B. Read the sentences. Complete each sentence with the noun form of the adjective in parentheses.**

1. I like the ________________ (simple) of this game. It's very easy to understand.
2. Sometimes the ideas in a game aren't much different from the ________________ (real) of an actual business.
3. I think our team can find an answer to the problem. We have a lot of ________________ (creative).
4. The ________________ (difficult) is going to be finding enough supply to meet the demand.

**C. Go online for more practice with suffixes.**

# SPEAKING

**At the end of this unit, you are going to work in a group to develop a simple educational board game. As part of the game development, you will have to give instructions to the players.**

## Grammar Imperative verbs

Use affirmative and negative **imperatives** to give instructions and directions.

For affirmative imperatives use the base form of the verb.

**Use** five lemons and four cups of sugar.
Now **watch** the screen.

For negative imperatives, use **do not** or **don't** + **the base form of the verb**. *Don't* is more common when speaking.

**Don't charge** 25 cents.

In imperative sentences, *you* is "understood" as the subject of the verb. We don't usually say or write the word *you*. However, when you are giving a long list of instructions, using *you* from time to time is polite.

*Next, **you** click OK.*

**A. Complete the conversation. Use imperatives. Then practice the conversation with a partner.**

**Khalid:** _______________ (1. help (affirmative)) me set up this board game, please.

**Max:** OK. How do we set it up? Please _______________ (2. show (affirmative)) me the instructions.

**Khalid:** _______________ (3. use (negative)) the instructions. I can tell you how to do it. Just _______________ (4. watch (affirmative)) me.

**Max:** Oh, I see. _______________ (5. give (affirmative)) me the question cards and I can sort them.

**Khalid:** _______________ (6. sort (negative)) them just yet. First, we need to put all the pieces on the board.

**Max:** I have an idea. You _______________ (7. work (affirmative)) on the pieces, and I can find the score sheet.

**B.** **Work with a partner. Tell your partner how to do something. Use imperatives. Choose one of the topics below or use your own idea.**

| How to buy something at a store<br>How to go online<br>How to learn a new word<br>How to make lemonade<br>How to sell something at a yard sale |
|---|

**C.** **Go online for more practice with imperative verbs.**

**D.** **Go online for the grammar expansion.**

## Pronunciation | Word stress

**Tip for Success**

Learning the correct pronunciation of a long word helps you remember the word. Then you will say it with the same stress and rhythm every time you use it.

The position of a stressed syllable varies in words with three or more syllables.

Notice where the main **stress** is in these words. For words that end in *-tion*, stress the syllable before the suffix.

| 1st syllable | 2nd syllable | 4th syllable |
|---|---|---|
| **lem**-on-ade | re-**mem**-ber | i-mag-i-**na**-tion |

There are some patterns that can help you decide which syllable to stress. For example, words ending with the suffix *-(c)ity* stress the syllable before the suffix.

ac-**tiv**-i-ty    sim-**pli**-ci-ty

Words with the suffix *-(t)y* usually have the stress on the first syllable.

**diff**-i-cul-ty    **hon**-es-ty

Sometimes you have to look up a word in the dictionary or ask someone to say the word to learn the correct pronunciation. When someone sees a new word, he or she often asks another person, "How do you pronounce this word?"

**A.** **Listen to the words. Where is the stress? Underline the stressed syllable.**

| 3-syllable words | 4-syllable words | 5- and 6-syllable words |
|---|---|---|
| introd<u>uce</u> | original | university |
| expensive | competition | originality |
| estimate | kindergarten | creativity |

**B. Listen to the words. Then repeat them. Use the correct stress.**

1. honesty
2. popularity
3. creativity
4. environment
5. reality
6. developer
7. calculate
8. history

**C. Go online for more practice with word stress.**

## Speaking Skill Giving instructions

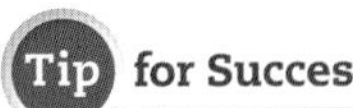

Stop from time to time and check that listeners understand your instructions. Ask a specific question or say something like, "Are you with me so far?"

When you're giving **instructions** about how to do something, first give a general description of the task. For example, to tell someone how to play a game, give some general information about the game and say what the object of the game is. Then present the steps in the correct order. Use phrases like these to make your instructions clear.

**The object of the game is to** make a profit.
**Here's how to** buy supplies and make the lemonade.

Use order words and phrases to make the sequence of instructions clear.

**First**, estimate the demand for lemonade.
**Next**, buy paper cups, lemons, sugar, and ice on the supply screen.
**After that**, you need to figure out how many lemons to use.
**Finally**, click OK to start selling your lemonade.

**A. Listen to the conversation about bowling. Complete the conversation with the words and phrases that make the instructions clear. Then practice the conversation with a partner.**

Bowling

**Mi-rae:** Is this your first time bowling? Don't worry. I can tell you how the game works.

**Liana:** OK. What do we do?

**Mi-rae:** Do you see those white things? They're called pins. The ____________(1) of the game is to knock them down with a ball. You roll the ball down the lane to hit them.

**Liana:** That sounds easy. What do I do first?

**Mi-rae:** ____________(2), choose a ball. Pick one that isn't too heavy for you.

**Liana:** OK. I think I'm going to use this ball. I really like the color. What do I do ________ (3)?

**Mi-rae:** ________ (4), you hold the ball with your fingers in the holes. ________ (5), you stand in front of the lane. Do you understand so far?

**Liana:** Yes. I get it so far. ________ (6) what do I do? Do I roll it with both hands?

**Mi-rae:** No, the ________ (7) is to roll it with one hand. ________ (8), try to roll it down the middle of the lane.

**Liana:** OK. Wow! I knocked down all the pins!

**Mi-rae:** Great! That's called a strike. You're going to be good at bowling!

Hide and seek

**B. Read the instructions about how to play hide and seek. Put the instructions in the correct order. Write 1 to 5 next to the sentences.**

___ Then, the other players hide while the seeker counts.

___ Finally, players try to return to the base. A player who is tagged, or touched, by the seeker loses.

___ Second, the seeker stands at the base, closes his or her eyes, and counts to 20.

_1_ First, choose one player in the group to seek, or look for, the other players.

___ Next, the seeker tries to find the hidden players.

**C. Go online for more practice with giving instructions.**

## Unit Assignment Develop a board game

**In this section, you are going to develop an educational board game that can help people in their real lives. You will then present it to the class. As you prepare your game, think about the Unit Question, "How can games compare to real life?" Use information from Listening 1, Listening 2, the unit video, and your work in this unit to support your presentation. Refer to the Self-Assessment checklist on page 88.**

## CONSIDER THE IDEAS

**A. Read these tips about creating board games.**

### How to Develop a Board Game

To develop a game, it's a good idea to work with two or three other people. A group creates more ideas, and you can test the game to see how it's working. Here are a few points to help you get started.

- First, think of a theme (main topic) for your game. It's usually more interesting if it's about a real-life situation or problem, such as business, education, travel, or family life.
- Next, narrow the topic so that it is something that is easily understood by the game players.
- Decide what the object of the game is. How does someone win the game?
- Then, decide on a design for the game. This includes the "path" for moving around the board. Draw the board on paper.
- After that, write the rules for the game. Don't make your game too complicated.
- Make any other things you need for the game, like game pieces or numbered cards.
- Test the game. Make sure that it is easy to play.
- Finally, have other people try the game to see what changes you need to make.

The most important thing is to make the game fun and easy to learn. You want people to like your game.

**B. Work in a group. Answer the questions.**

1. Why is it better to work in a group to develop a game?
2. What kind of themes does the website suggest?
3. What are the most important things to do when you develop a game?

## PREPARE AND SPEAK

**A.** **GATHER IDEAS** **Work in a group. Agree on one game theme from the list below or think of your own. Then narrow your theme so it is easy for game players to understand.**

| |
|---|
| a game that helps people learn English |
| a game about some kind of business |
| a game about traveling in foreign countries |

**Example:**

Theme: A game that helps people learn English
Narrowed: 25 irregular verbs in English

**B.** **ORGANIZE IDEAS** **With your group, create a simple board game using the tips on page 87. Follow these steps.**

1. Discuss and plan the game. Remember to make the game very simple.
2. Gather materials you need. Use things in the classroom for markers and game pieces.
3. Make small pieces of paper and number them from 1 to 10. Players can pick a card to find out how many spaces their markers should move.
4. Draw the board on a piece of paper.
5. Write a short list of rules for the game.

**C.** **SPEAK** **Work with another group. Explain the rules of your game to the other group. Have them play your game. Then learn the other group's game and play it. Refer to the Self-Assessment checklist below before you begin.**

**Go online for your alternate Unit Assignment.**

## CHECK AND REFLECT

**A.** **CHECK** **Think about the Unit Assignment as you complete the Self-Assessment checklist.**

| SELF-ASSESSMENT | | |
|---|---|---|
| Yes | No | |
| ☐ | ☐ | I was able to speak easily about the topic. |
| ☐ | ☐ | My partner, group, class understood me. |
| ☐ | ☐ | I used imperative verbs. |
| ☐ | ☐ | I used vocabulary from the unit. |
| ☐ | ☐ | I gave instructions. |
| ☐ | ☐ | I used correct word stress. |

**B. REFLECT** **Go to the Online Discussion Board to discuss these questions.**

1. What is something new you learned in this unit?
2. Look back at the Unit Question—How can games compare to real life? Is your answer different now than when you started this unit? If yes, how is it different? Why?

## TRACK YOUR SUCCESS

**Circle the words and phrases you have learned in this unit.**

| **Nouns** | **Verbs** | **Adjectives** |
|---|---|---|
| clue | calculate | instant |
| demand | estimate AWL | original |
| developer | realize | **Phrasal Verb** |
| loss | update | figure out |
| object | | **Phrase** |
| profit | | sold out |
| supplies | | |
| version AWL | | |

Oxford 3000™ words

AWL Academic Word List

**Check (✓) the skills you learned. If you need more work on a skill, refer to the page(s) in parentheses.**

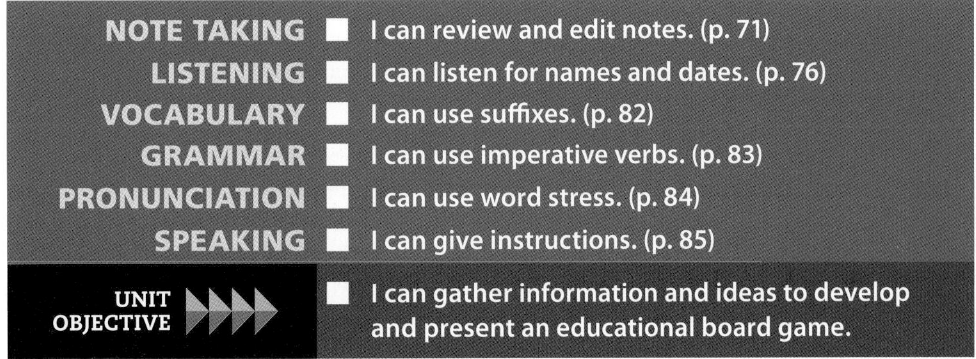

| | |
|---|---|
| NOTE TAKING | ■ I can review and edit notes. (p. 71) |
| LISTENING | ■ I can listen for names and dates. (p. 76) |
| VOCABULARY | ■ I can use suffixes. (p. 82) |
| GRAMMAR | ■ I can use imperative verbs. (p. 83) |
| PRONUNCIATION | ■ I can use word stress. (p. 84) |
| SPEAKING | ■ I can give instructions. (p. 85) |
| UNIT OBJECTIVE | ■ I can gather information and ideas to develop and present an educational board game. |

# AUDIO TRACK LIST

Audio can be found in the *iQ Online* Media Center. Go to iQOnlinePractice.com. Click on the Media Center. Choose to stream or download the audio file you select. Not all audio files are available for download.

| Page | Track Name: Q2e_02_LS_ |
|---|---|
| 3 | U01_Q_Classroom.mp3 |
| 5 | U01_NoteTakingSkill_ActivityB.mp3 |
| 7 | U01_Listening1_ActivityA.mp3 |
| 7 | U01_Listening1_ActivityB.mp3 |
| 7 | U01_Listening1_ActivityD.mp3 |
| 9 | U01_ListeningSkill_ActivityA.mp3 |
| 10 | U01_ListeningSkill_ActivityB.mp3 |
| 11 | U01_Listening2_ActivityA.mp3 |
| 12 | U01_Listening2_ActivityB.mp3 |
| 12 | U01_Listening2_ActivityD.mp3 |
| 17 | U01_Grammar_ActivityB.mp3 |
| 17 | U01_Pronunciation_Example1.mp3 |
| 17 | U01_Pronunciation_Example2.mp3 |
| 17 | U01_Pronunciation_ActivityA.mp3 |
| 20 | U01_UnitAssignment.mp3 |
| 25 | U02_Q_Classroom.mp3 |
| 27 | U02_NoteTakingSkill_ActivityB.mp3 |
| 29 | U02_Listening1_ActivityB.mp3 |
| 29 | U02_Listening1_ActivityC.mp3 |
| 30 | U02_Listening1_ActivityD.mp3 |
| 32 | U02_ListeningSkill_ActivityA.mp3 |
| 32 | U02_ListeningSkill_ActivityB.mp3 |
| 34 | U02_Listening2_ActivityA.mp3 |
| 34 | U02_Listening2_ActivityB.mp3 |
| 34 | U02_Listening2_ActivityC.mp3 |
| 35 | U02_Listening2_ActivityD.mp3 |
| 40 | U02_Pronunciation_Examples.mp3 |
| 40 | U02_Pronunciation_ActivityA.mp3 |
| 40 | U02_Pronunciation_ActivityB.mp3 |
| 40 | U02_Pronunciation_ActivityC.mp3 |
| 41 | U02_SpeakingSkill_ActivityA.mp3 |
| 47 | U03_Q_Classroom.mp3 |
| 51 | U03_ListeningSkill_ActivityE_Part1.mp3 |
| 51 | U03_ListeningSkill_ActivityE_Part2.mp3 |
| 51 | U03_ListeningSkill_ActivityE_Part3.mp3 |
| 51 | U03_Listening1_ActivityA.mp3 |
| 52 | U03_Listening1_ActivityC.mp3 |
| 53 | U03_Listening1_ActivityE.mp3 |
| 54 | U03_NoteTakingSkill_ActivityA.mp3 |
| 56 | U03_Listening2_ActivityA.mp3 |
| 56 | U03_Listening2_ActivityB.mp3 |
| 57 | U03_Listening2_ActivityD.mp3 |
| 57 | U03_Listening2_ActivityE.mp3 |
| 62 | U03_Pronunciation_Examples.mp3 |
| 62 | U03_Pronunciation_ActivityB.mp3 |
| 62 | U03_Pronunciation_ActivityC.mp3 |

| Page | Track Name: Q2e_02_LS_ |
|---|---|
| 68 | U04_Q_Classroom.mp3 |
| 71 | U04_NoteTakingSkill_ActivityA.mp3 |
| 73 | U04_Listening1_ActivityA.mp3 |
| 74 | U04_Listening1_ActivityB.mp3 |
| 74 | U04_Listening1_ActivityD.mp3 |
| 76 | U04_ListeningSkill_ActivityA.mp3 |
| 78 | U04_Listening2_ActivityA.mp3 |
| 79 | U04_Listening2_ActivityB.mp3 |
| 84 | U04_Pronunciation_Examples.mp3 |
| 84 | U04_Pronunciation_ActivityA.mp3 |
| 85 | U04_Pronunciation_ActivityB.mp3 |
| 85 | U04_SpeakingSkill_ActivityA.mp3 |
| 91 | U05_Q_Classroom.mp3 |
| 93 | U05_NoteTakingSkill_ActivityA.mp3 |
| 95 | U05_Listening1_ActivityA.mp3 |
| 95 | U05_Listening1_ActivityB.mp3 |
| 95 | U05_Listening1_ActivityC.mp3 |
| 96 | U05_Listening1_ActivityD.mp3 |
| 98 | U05_ListeningSkill_ActivityA.mp3 |
| 98 | U05_ListeningSkill_ActivityB.mp3 |
| 101 | U05_Listening2_ActivityA.mp3 |
| 101 | U05_Listening2_ActivityB.mp3 |
| 101 | U05_Listening2_ActivityD.mp3 |
| 102 | U05_Listening2_ActivityE.mp3 |
| 107 | U05_Pronunciation_Examples.mp3 |
| 107 | U05_Pronunciation_ActivityA.mp3 |
| 108 | U05_SpeakingSkill_ActivityA.mp3 |
| 113 | U06_Q_Classroom.mp3 |
| 115 | U06_NoteTakingSkill_ActivityB.mp3 |
| 117 | U06_Listening1_ActivityA.mp3 |
| 118 | U06_Listening1_ActivityB.mp3 |
| 118 | U06_Listening1_ActivityD.mp3 |
| 120 | U06_ListeningSkill_ActivityA.mp3 |
| 120 | U06_ListeningSkill_ActivityB.mp3 |
| 123 | U06_Listening2_ActivityA.mp3 |
| 123 | U06_Listening2_ActivityB.mp3 |
| 123 | U06_Listening2_ActivityD.mp3 |
| 127 | U06_VocabularySkill_ActivityA.mp3 |
| 130 | U06_Pronunciation_Examples.mp3 |
| 130 | U06_Pronunciation_ActivityA.mp3 |
| 136 | U07_Q_Classroom.mp3 |
| 140 | U07_Listening1_ActivityB.mp3 |
| 141 | U07_Listening1_ActivityC.mp3 |
| 143 | U07_ListeningSkill_ActivityA_Part1.mp3 |
| 143 | U07_ListeningSkill_ActivityA_Part2.mp3 |

| Page | Track Name: Q2e_02_LS_ |
|---|---|
| 143 | U07_ListeningSkill_ActivityA_Part3.mp3 |
| 144 | U07_ListeningSkill_ActivityB.mp3 |
| 145 | U07_NoteTakingSkill_ActivityB.mp3 |
| 145 | U07_NoteTakingSkill_ActivityC.mp3 |
| 147 | U07_Listening2_ActivityB.mp3 |
| 147 | U07_Listening2_ActivityD.mp3 |
| 152 | U07_Pronunciation_Examples.mp3 |
| 153 | U07_Pronunciation_ActivityA.mp3 |
| 154 | U07_SpeakingSkill_ActivityB_Part1.mp3 |
| 154 | U07_SpeakingSkill_ActivityB_Part2.mp3 |
| 155 | U07_UnitAssignment.mp3 |
| 158 | U08_Q_Classroom.mp3 |
| 162 | U08_Listening1_ActivityA.mp3 |
| 163 | U08_Listening1_ActivityB.mp3 |
| 163 | U08_Listening1_ActivityC.mp3 |
| 164 | U08_Listening1_ActivityD.mp3 |
| 165 | U08_ListeningSkill_ActivityA.mp3 |
| 165 | U08_ListeningSkill_ActivityB.mp3 |
| 168 | U08_Listening2_ActivityA.mp3 |
| 169 | U08_Listening2_ActivityC.mp3 |
| 169 | U08_Listening2_ActivityE.mp3 |
| 174 | U08_Grammar_ActivityA.mp3 |
| 175 | U08_Pronunciation_Examples.mp3 |
| 175 | U08_Pronunciation_ActivityA.mp3 |
| 176 | U08_Pronunciation_ActivityC.mp3 |
| 177 | U08_SpeakingSkill_ActivityA_Part1.mp3 |
| 177 | U08_SpeakingSkill_ActivityA_Part2.mp3 |
| 177 | U08_SpeakingSkill_ActivityA_Part3.mp3 |

# AUTHORS AND CONSULTANTS

## Author

**Margaret Brooks** has a Master of Arts in Teaching degree from Harvard University. She worked for many years as teacher and administrator in a variety of English language-teaching programs in the Dominican Republic and Costa Rica. This experience included serving as a professor at the Autonomous University of Santo Domingo and working with a private company to develop specialized language courses for businesses in Costa Rica. She has always had a lively interest in the development of classroom materials and innovative teaching methods.

## Series Consultants

### ONLINE INTEGRATION

**Chantal Hemmi** holds an Ed.D. TEFL and is a Japan-based teacher trainer and curriculum designer. Since leaving her position as Academic Director of the British Council in Tokyo, she has been teaching at the Center for Language Education and Research at Sophia University on an EAP/CLIL program offered for undergraduates. She delivers lectures and teacher trainings throughout Japan, Indonesia, and Malaysia.

### COMMUNICATIVE GRAMMAR

**Nancy Schoenfeld** holds an M.A. in TESOL from Biola University in La Mirada, California, and has been an English language instructor since 2000. She has taught ESL in California and Hawaii, and EFL in Thailand and Kuwait. She has also trained teachers in the United States and Indonesia. Her interests include teaching vocabulary, extensive reading, and student motivation. She is currently an English Language Instructor at Kuwait University.

### WRITING

**Marguerite Ann Snow** holds a Ph.D. in Applied Linguistics from UCLA. She teaches in the TESOL M.A. program in the Charter College of Education at California State University, Los Angeles. She was a Fulbright scholar in Hong Kong and Cyprus. In 2006, she received the President's Distinguished Professor award at Cal State, LA. She has trained EFL teachers in Algeria, Argentina, Brazil, Egypt, Libya, Morocco, Pakistan, Peru, Spain, and Turkey. She is the author/editor of publications in the areas of integrated content, English for academic purposes, and standards for English teaching and learning. She recently served as a co-editor of *Teaching English as a Second or Foreign Language* (4th ed.).

### VOCABULARY

**Cheryl Boyd Zimmerman** is a Professor at California State University, Fullerton. She specializes in second-language vocabulary acquisition, an area in which she is widely published. She teaches graduate courses on second-language acquisition, culture, vocabulary, and the fundamentals of TESOL and is a frequent invited speaker on topics related to vocabulary teaching and learning. She is the author of *Word Knowledge: A Vocabulary Teacher's Handbook* and Series Director of *Inside Reading*, *Inside Writing*, and *Inside Listening and Speaking*, all published by Oxford University Press.

### ASSESSMENT

**Lawrence J. Zwier** holds an M.A. in TESL from the University of Minnesota. He is currently the Associate Director for Curriculum Development at the English Language Center at Michigan State University in East Lansing. He has taught ESL/EFL in the United States, Saudi Arabia, Malaysia, Japan, and Singapore.

UNIVERSITY PRESS

198 Madison Avenue
New York, NY 10016 USA

Great Clarendon Street, Oxford, OX2 6DP, United Kingdom

Oxford University Press is a department of the University of Oxford. It furthers the University's objective of excellence in research, scholarship, and education by publishing worldwide. Oxford is a registered trade mark of Oxford University Press in the UK and in certain other countries



First published in 2015
2019 2018 2017 2016 2015
10 9 8 7 6 5 4 3 2 1



Director, ELT New York: Laura Pearson
Head of Adult, ELT New York: Stephanie Karras
Publisher: Sharon Sargent
Managing Editor: Mariel DeKranis
Development Editor: Eric Zuarino
Executive Art and Design Manager: Maj-Britt Hagsted
Design Project Manager: Debbie Lofaso
Content Production Manager: Julie Armstrong
Senior Production Artist: Elissa Santos
Image Manager: Trisha Masterson
Image Editor: Liaht Ziskind
Production Coordinator: Brad Tucker

ISBN: 978 0 19 481878 0 Student Book 2A with iQ Online pack
ISBN: 978 0 19 481879 7 Student Book 2A as pack component
ISBN: 978 0 19 481802 5 iQ Online student website

Printed in China
This book is printed on paper from certified and well-managed sources.

ACKNOWLEDGEMENTS

*Illustrations by*: p. 4 Barb Bastian; p. 26 Jean Tuttle; p. 27 5W Infographics; p. 48 Karen Minot; p. 70 Claudia Carlson; p. 114 Barb Bastian; p. 138 Barb Bastian; p. 160 Bill Smith Group; p. 176 Claudia Carlson.

*We would also like to thank the following for permission to reproduce the following photographs*: Cover: David Pu'u/Corbis; Video Vocabulary (used throughout the book): Oleksiy Mark / Shutterstock; p. 2 Helene ROCHE Photography/ Alamy; p. 2/3 Sofiaworld/Shutterstock; p. 3 vahekatrjya/iStockphoto (chair); p3 Dmytro Grankin/Alamy (building); p. 5 chuvipro/Getty Images; p. 6 Arcaid Images/Alamy; p. 7 John Warburton-Lee Photography/Alamy; p. 12 Daniele Zacchi/Stefano Boeri Architetti; p. 19 Niall Cotton/Alamy; p. 20 jl661227/Shutterstock; p. 24 Parawat Isarangura Na Ayudhaya/Alamy; p. 24/25 Africa Studio/Shutterstock; p. 25 Marie C Fields/Shutterstock (brush); p. 25 pfb1/iStockphoto (hydrant); p. 26 Robert Dant/Getty Images; p. 29 thumb/iStockphoto (hat); p. 29 Jason Bazzano/Alamy (katydid); p. 29 Chris Mattison/Frank Lane Picture Agency (frog); p. 29 Chris Mattison/ Frank Lane Picture Agency (blue frog); p. 31 Purestock/Oxford University Press (butterfly); p. 31 Photoshot/Alamy (fox); p. 31 Lorne Chapman/Alamy (zebra); p. 31 Jared Hobbs/Getty Images (snake); p. 31 Steven J. Kazlowski/ Alamy (white fox); p. 32 Konrad Wothe/Minden Pictures/Frank Lane Picture Agency; p. 34 Roger Brooks/Beateworks/Corbis UK Ltd. (desk); p. 34 Satoshi Asakawa/Kengo Kuma & Associates (bamboo); p. 34 Peter Horree/Alamy (Hundertwasser); p. 36 Hemis /Alamy (coloured building); p. 36 Nacasa & Partners Inc./Artechnic (rounded house); p. 38 ZSSD/Frank Lane Picture Agency; p. 42 Bildagentur Zoonar GmbH/Shutterstock (colourful houses); p. 42 imageBROKER/Alamy (hut); p. 42 PANAGIOTIS KARAPANAGIOTIS/Alamy (white house); p. 42 GFC Collection/Alamy (red roof); p. 46 Image Source/ Getty Images; p. 47 ryasick/iStockphoto (mobile); p. 47 rnl/Shutterstock (gifts); p. 51 Chris Ryan/Getty Images; p. 56 MBI/Oxford University Press; p. 62 Bettmann/Corbis UK Ltd. (Roosevelt); p. 62 Corbis UK Ltd. (Kennedy); p. 69 TopPhoto via AP Images; p. 71 Judith Collins/Alamy (monopoly); p. 71 Thomas E Forsyth/The Landlord's Game (landlord); p. 73 David Pleacher (first crossword); p. 73 Lisa Solonynko/Alamy (crossword pen); p. 76 Zooid Pictures; p. 78 David Sacks/Getty Images (yard sale); p. 78 www.impulsecorp.com/Impulse Communications Inc. (lemonade inventory); p. 78 www.impulsecorp.com/Impulse Communications Inc. (lemonade price); p. 85 Alex Segre/Alamy; p. 86 ArtBox Images RM/Getty Images; p. 90 Julia Ivantsova/Shutterstock (rings); p. 90 Rob Lewine/Tetra Images/ Corbis/Corbis UK Ltd. (family); p. 91 Imagesbybarbara/iStockphoto (album cover); p. 91 STOCKFOLIO/Alamy (album); p. 94 Rebecca Emery/Getty Images; p. 100 Andrew Johnson/iStockphoto (DNA); p. 100 AKG-images (family); p. 112 Jose Luis Pelaez Inc/Blend Im/Corbis UK Ltd.; p. 112/113 Riccardo_Mojana/iStockphoto; p. 113 evemilla/iStockphoto (yarn); p. 113 Africa Studio/Shutterstock (gardening); p. 117 Peter Holmes/Getty Images (tools); p. 117 Stockbyte/Getty Images (students); p. 121 Scratch/Lifelong Kindergarden Group; p. 122 age fotostock /Superstock Ltd. (pearls); p. 122 Tony Hobbs/Alamy (fair); p. 125 Jekaterina Nikitina/Getty Images; p. 136/137 Roger Bamber/Alamy; p. 138 Francesc Muntada/Corbis UK Ltd.; p. 140 Ros Drinkwater/Alamy; p. 146 All Canada Photos/Alamy; p. 153 David Chapman/ Alamy; p. 155 2013 AFP/Getty Images (garbage men); p. 155 Pat Tuson/ Alamy (bag); p. 158/159 Yuriy Rudyy/Shutterstock; p. 160 Stuwdamdorp/ Alamy (dishes); p. 160 Photodisc/Oxford University Press (watering); p. 162 Photodisc/Oxford University Press; p. 164 AfriPics.com/Alamy; p. 168 Big Pants productions/Alamy (soap); p. 168 dbimages/Alamy (playground); p. 168 Imagebroker/Alamy (mud); p. 170 Emel Yenigelen/Getty Images (pain); p. 170 ballyscanlon/Getty Images (sneezing).